# Copywriting

The Marketing Series is one of the most comprehensive collections of books in marketing and sales available from the UK today.

Published by Butterworth-Heinemann on behalf of The Chartered Institute of Marketing, the series is divided into three distinct groups: *Student* (fulfilling the needs of those taking the Institute's certificate and diploma qualifications; *Professional Development* (for those on formal or self-study vocational training programmes); and *Practitioner* (presented in a more informal, motivating and highly practical manner for the busy marketer).

Formed in 1911, The Central Institute of Marketing is now the largest professional marketing management body in Europe with over 60,000 members located worldwide. Its primary objectives are focused on the development of awareness and understanding of marketing throughout UK industry and commerce and in the raising of standards of professionalism in the education, training and practice of this key business discipline.

## Books in the series

# Copywriting

**Moi Ali**

*Published on behalf of*
*The Chartered Institute of Marketing*

To Spike's little brother or sister

Butterworth-Heinemann Ltd
Linacre House, Jordan Hill, Oxford OX2 8DP

A member of the Reed Elsevier plc group

OXFORD    BOSTON    JOHANNESBURG
MELBOURNE    NEW DELHI    SINGAPORE

First published 1997

**British Library Cataloguing in Publication Data**
Ali, M.
    Copywriting. – (CIM practitioner series)
    1. Advertising copy
    I. Title
    659.1'32


ISBN 0 7506 3510 X

Typeset by David Gregson Associates, Beccles, Suffolk
Printed and bound in Great Britain by Biddles Ltd, Guildford and King's Lynn

# Contents

# Introduction

It must be hell being a Weight Watchers tutor. Class after class of chubbies scrutinizing every inch of your body for excess fat. They not unreasonably expect you to have the body beautiful: after all, how can you help them get slim if you cannot yourself achieve a svelte physique? I suspect that writing on copywriting is not unlike that. You will expect me to demonstrate through my own writing all the things I will be urging you to do. You will demand writing excellence. You will be more critical of my style than if I were writing a book on gardening or chess. I will be thoroughly under the spotlight. That's fine, because one of the best ways of becoming a better copywriter is to analyse and criticize the work of others. Learn from what they get wrong. Copy what they get right.

Few business people and in-house marketers have formal copywriting training, yet most are required to write marketing material. Does this sound like you? It used to be me too. I learned copywriting the hard way (by trial and error over a number of years) but I'd like you to learn it the easy (or perhaps I should say 'easier') way. This book will give you the training you (and I) never had. It condenses years of experience into a volume that can be read start to finish in the time it takes to travel from Portsmouth to Edinburgh by train. So if you want to short-circuit the learning curve, this book is for you.

It is split into two parts. Part 1 covers theory, although it is in no way theoretical or jargony. The book is a plain English, step-by-step, nuts-and-bolts account of how to write for marketing. It covers the do's and don'ts, asks a range of professionals for their tips and insights, looks at planning, audiences and styles, and reveals the copywriter's tricks and techniques. Part 2 looks chapter by chapter at the main pieces of marketing material you are likely to have to write – direct mail, press ads, sales letters, etc. – and explains how to produce the very best of each.

This book will not transform you into the William Shakespeare of marketing copy. If only it could! But it will dramatically improve your marketing copy. It will guide, advise and encourage you. It will help you develop and fine tune your writing ability quickly and efficiently, fast-tracking you towards your ultimate goal of really great marketing material. That's what's on offer from this book, but the really magic ingredient is *you*. The book will provide the advice, but it is up to you to throw in the time, enthusiasm and commitment to improve your copywriting. You need to practise and practise again. You must put in the effort. If you are willing, together we can be a powerful team. So read on and watch yourself get better and better.

## About the author

Moi Ali runs her own communications consultancy, The Pink Anglia Public Relations Company, which specializes in public relations, communications and marketing services for voluntary organizations and small businesses. She has 15 years' experience in public relations and promotional marketing, working in-house for companies and voluntary organizations, as well as in PR/marketing consultancies. Moi has tackled a wide variety of copywriting assignments, ranging from leaflets and annual reports to major works – including three books to date. Although she has no formal training as a copywriter, she has over the years gained considerable experience in writing for marketing. Her aim in this book is to condense those years of experience into the following pages, passing on to readers the knowledge she has built up over a decade and a half.

# PART 1

PART 1

# 1 Second-rate copy makes for second-rate marketing

In this chapter you will see why good copy is so important and what you stand to lose if you get it wrong. I will look at the fear and anxiety experienced by many people who have to write marketing copy, and there will be an opportunity to assess your current writing ability.

It amazes me how so many business and marketing people put enormous effort into selecting the right mailing list, choosing the right media for their advertising, or the best photographs for a brochure, only to let poor copy spoil their hard work. Well-targeted mailings or wonderful-looking publicity materials will fail in their purpose if they are badly written. Your entire marketing campaign will be undermined. All the time, effort and money invested in a campaign will be wasted. That's because good marketing copy is a must. It can boost your marketing activity in so many ways. Here are just a few reasons why you should strive for excellence:

- Good, clear copy is essential for effective communication, averting the kind of misunderstanding that leads to ill will between a customer and an organization/company
- Good copy persuades and influences
- Good copy leads to sales
- Good copy enhances the image of a company
- Good copy can help you distinguish yourself from your competitors
- Good copy can be used as a powerful weapon to help you beat off the competition
- Often the written material a company produces is the first or only contact someone will have with them. It will be used as the basis for deciding whether the customer wants further contact: the corporate 'you' will be judged on the basis of the copy. Get it wrong and you will lose customers
- Today's consumers are more sophisticated than those of our parents' generation. They expect the design and content of marketing material to be of a higher quality
- Good copy gets read: bad copy gets scrapped
- Good copy can give you a powerful competitive advantage

It is obvious, then, that good copy is really important. But if it is so obvious, why is it that so much poor copy makes it into print? There are two possible reasons.

The first is that many marketing and business people simply underestimate the vital contribution that good copy can make to a marketing programme. They are so preoccupied with creative design, clever mailshots or eye-catching exhibitions that they overlook the foundation stone upon which all of these are built: good copy. Sometimes the words are almost an after-thought, with an over-emphasis on the more glamorous and tangible aspects of a campaign, at the expense of good copy.

Another explanation as to why poor copy makes it into print is that many people have difficulty in telling bad copy from good copy. They do not find it easy to understand what makes some writing powerful and other writing painful. Such people are particularly blind when it comes to their own writing, with some quite unable to see the inadequacies in their own work. That may seem rather a damning judgement, but I have come across many people like this.

Then there are the people like you. You are persuaded of the value of good copy and aware that your own skills in this area could be more polished. You want to find out how you can start writing great copy.

In theory all of us should be able to write well. After all, we spent years in school studying grammar, spelling, and punctuation. In practice it was probably those English lessons that turned many of us off writing. All that syntax, those complicated rules about sentence construction, verbs, adverbs, prepositions. The good news is that you can learn to write good marketing copy relatively pain-free. Much of what you had drummed into you in English lessons can be forgotten (within limits!). Together we can make a clean start that is not blighted by distant memories of school compositions.

My aim is to liberate you from the stifling influence of your English teacher. To free the creativity within you. To unlock your writing power. So shake off the belief that you can't write. You can. All you need is plenty of practice, a little confidence building, and a liberal helping of trade secrets. Before long you will be writing powerful sales letters, persuasive adverts, and really readable promotional material. Just follow the easy steps described, pick up some tips along the way, and overnight (well almost!) you will be writing more effective marketing material.

## Overcome the fear

Many people do not believe that they can write well. Some are too afraid even to try. Fear prevents most of us from taking up dangerous sports, yet unlike daredevil antics, copywriting is not potentially lethal. Nevertheless, it is frequently feared as much as if it were. Jumping off the Clifton Suspension Bridge supported by an elastic band might cause your death: having a go at drafting a press advert will not. So put any fears and anxieties to one side. You cannot be harmed by having a go.

Start by recognizing any fears or anxieties you have about writing. You are quite normal. A straw poll of a dozen of my acquaintances revealed that eleven of them found writing promotional material both difficult and time-consuming. So accept that you are not alone and cast off your anxiety: it's nothing more than a barrier preventing you from fulfilling your potential. Concentrate on boosting your writing skills and you will find that your confidence grows.

I am assuming you think your writing can be improved; that's why you are reading this book. Too many people think that good writers are born. It's a very easy excuse for them to give up without trying. True, a few people are blessed with a natural ability to write: the rest of us have to learn. But learn we can. So don't write yourself off as a no-hoper. There is an art to writing: few of us could turn out work of a quality to match Charles Dickens, George Eliot, or the other great writers of fiction, but writing for marketing is a different kettle of fish. In large part it is a skill that can be learnt by any reasonably intelligent adult. Even you! Once you've acquired the skill, it's all down to creativity. That's the factor that distinguishes the technically competent from the great. This book will give you the technical competence and it will nurture any innate creativity you have. In short, it will turn you into a better copywriter.

But let's start with where you are now. Begin by assessing your current writing ability as a benchmark. You can reassess it at the end of the book to see if you have gained in skill and confidence. If this book is worth the paper it's written on, you will see an overall improvement in your writing ability.

Work through the following questions. Select only one answer for each question, then tot up your score at the end.

## Current writing ability: self-assessment test

1  I would rate my writing ability as:
   (a)  Poor
   (b)  Slightly below average
   (c)  Average
   (d)  Slightly above average
   (e)  Good
   (f)  Excellent

2  I find getting started:
   (a)  Almost impossible
   (b)  Very difficult
   (c)  Quite difficult
   (d)  Hard but not insurmountable
   (e)  Reasonably easy
   (f)  Very easy

3  When I am asked to write some marketing material I feel:
   (a)  A sense of dread and panic
   (b)  Worried that I will make a mess of it
   (c)  That it will be a struggle, but I will be able to come up with something, however second-rate
   (d)  That I will do an OK job, but not a great one
   (e)  That I will be able to produce a good piece of work
   (f)  That it will be a doddle and the output will be great

4  I think that the marketing material I write is:
   (a)  Dreadful
   (b)  Poor
   (c)  Average
   (d)  Good but could be improved
   (e)  Above average
   (f)  Excellent

5  When it comes to words and language:
   (a)  I have no interest in words and how they work – indeed I never give words so much as a passing thought
   (b)  I'm not that interested in words, but very occasionally I will look at an ad or brochure and wonder how the creators came up with the concept
   (c)  I have an average interest in words – no more and no less than an average marketing person
   (d)  I often look at/analyse/think about other people's creative work
   (e)  I love reading and thinking about professional copy and find myself doing it all the time
   (f)  I am very interested in words, indeed I find language fascinating

6  When it comes to writing marketing material (sales letters, press ads, brochures, annual reports):
   (a)  I find it difficult to write anything and always feel dissatisfied with the end result
   (b)  I have trouble getting started and rarely like the finished material

(c) I can write some types of marketing material to a reasonable standard, but find others more difficult

(d) I can write most types of material, but there's room for improvement across the board

(e) I am confident that I can tackle most assignments without too much difficulty and can produce good work

(f) I can turn my hand to anything with ease, always producing very good work

7 How long does it take you to write, say, a one-page sales letter, or some other short piece of marketing material, to a good standard?

(a) It takes me far far too long to get material written – perhaps three times too long. I pore over it and never feel that it is right

(b) It takes me a lot longer than it should, but I get there in the end

(c) I take a little longer than I should

(d) I am fairly quick, but I could be a bit faster

(e) I can produce good work faster than the average person

(f) I can turn out quality work quickly.

## Scores

Now add up your score. Award yourself:
One point for every (a) you ticked
Two for every (b)
Three for a (c)
Four for a (d)
Five for an (e)
Six for an (f)

## Assessment

Read the paragraph that refers to your score.

### 7–12

Either you really are as bad at writing as you think you are, or you have extremely low self-esteem! This is a poor score, but the good news is that it can only go up. There is much you can learn to enhance your skills and build your confidence. You should see a dramatic increase in your score by the end of the book.

### 13–19

You fall into the slightly below average category. Your writing is not that good, though it is far from bad. You don't find it easy to write

⌐ you are not too confident about the end result. Never fear. By the time you reach page 188 you will have bags more confidence and you will find getting started so much easier. You will also be happier with your output.

## 20–34

This is an average to above-average score. Your writing is fine, but there is room for improvement. You can get started and turn out acceptable work. However, you could be faster and a bit slicker. You will be by the end of the book.

## 35–42

You're either extremely talented or extremely conceited. If the former, you clearly have no need for this book: give it to someone else. And the latter? Consult a psychiatrist!

This test is semi-serious. It gives you a rough idea of where you stand in the scheme of things. Once you have worked your way through the book, repeat the test (it can be found reprinted at the end of the book). See how your confidence and ability have grown.

# 2 Planning and research

Before you put pen to paper, there is an important step in the copywriting process that it is advisable to take: the research stage. This involves looking at who you are writing for, what you want to say to them, and what action you hope they will take as a result. This chapter will take you step by step through this process.

Professional copywriters rarely sit down and write fluent, flowing and perfectly polished prose straight off. If only life were so simple! Certainly I did not turn out this book in a couple of weeks. I planned, researched, drafted and redrafted over many hard months. On a smaller scale, that's what is required with marketing copy too. You must clear the groundwork before you start to write. This involves giving consideration to:

- Audience – who you are writing for
- Purpose – what you hope to achieve through your writing
- Message – the benefits and unique selling points you need to convey

Only when you have completed this initial thinking, researching and planning stage can you begin to write. Many inexperienced copywriters feel failures because they cannot sit down with a blank sheet of paper (or, more likely, a clear VDU screen) and instantly churn out startlingly original and creative work. Once they realize that the planning stage is a vital precursor, they find that writing is so much easier.

The first step in the planning phase is to look at your audience.

## Audience

Start by considering who you are writing for. No professional writer can write meaningfully without regard to their audience. Each different audience will have distinct needs, interests and preferences. You can only define these once you have defined your audience. (Often you will find yourself writing not for one clearly defined audience but for a range of very diverse audiences. This is, clearly, a challenge.)

Before starting to write this book I knew that I would be writing for in-house marketing people, not for agency copywriters. As a result I have been able to tailor the content to meet the needs of the in-houser. There's no mention of art directors or creative teams because these are relevant only to agency staff. By knowing that I am writing for you, I can make this book relevant to you and to your situation as an in-house marketer. You, too, must remember your reader.

A common mistake in marketing material is to forget the reader. It is all too easily done. You find yourself so wrapped up with your company/organization, or with your products, that you completely overlook the poor old reader, struggling to make sense of it all (or, more likely, giving up and chucking your work in the bin). If you don't make a conscious effort to remember your reader, they won't remember you (or they will, but for all the wrong reasons). If you forget your reader, you might as well be talking to yourself. Talking to yourself is not communicating: talking to others is.

When you write to your great-aunt Tabitha, she's likely to want to read what you have to say, eager for news of her favourite niece or nephew. Unfortunately, the person reading your marketing material will not have your great-aunt's avid interest in you. Your reader may not be interested in you at all, or your company. Your job is to get them interested – quickly – and to keep them reading. It's a far from easy task, but you can make it easier by remembering your reader as you write. Your aim is riveted readers. Remember that riveted readers require riveting writing.

Let's say you are about to start work on some new promotional material. Begin by asking: 'Who will be reading it?'. Make sure your answer is as specific as possible. 'Business people' is too vague. Will they be managers? Self-employed? Running large companies? Small businesses? Mainly male? Female? Young? Old? If you have a very slick marketing operation, you should already have an accurate picture of your typical reader, in the form of your customer profile. This will be an enormous help to you. If you do not have this facility, do your own research. Find out as much as you can about your audience. Think about whether you know anyone who fits your target audience. Write for them. It is always easier to write for a real person than for an abstract classification such as 'AB males under 35'.

Try to get inside the head of your reader. What will make them sit up and take notice? What interests them? What situation are they in? How much time do they have to deal with your mailing or your advert? Are they being bombarded with similar material from other companies? Are they in a busy office with competing demands on their time? Are they retired, at home, and with loads of free time on their hands? Are they at home and stressed out looking after screaming children? Think about what they will be doing when they read your copy. Think how they will be feeling. Recall all of this when you come to write. If you ignore the needs of your audience, and the pressures on them, you cannot expect your copy to achieve its goal.

In general terms you will find that a particular group will have its own needs, wants, preferences and pressures. Take the example of a manager in a large company:

---

The manager: their situation
- Managers are busy people.
- Direct mail sent to managers is often opened by secretaries.
- Most managers receive lots of so-called 'junk mail' and unsolicited material.
- Most managers want to clear their in-trays. It is easier to bin complicated marketing material than read it.
- Managers usually have a great deal of professional reading to do – reports, trade publications, etc. You will be competing with this.

The manager: their needs
- Managers want the benefits to them clearly spelt out early on.
- They want relevant information – that will help them or their business.
- They want material tailored to their job/profession, so they know immediately that your communication is relevant.
- They need information that is short and to the point – they don't have time to wade through heavy copy.
- They want everything set out so it is easy to digest – lots of bullet points, boxes, callouts and so on.
- They don't want padding and puffery.
- They are happy with the use of their own trade jargon – but not with jargon they do not understand.

---

By contrast, look at the needs of a hobbyist/enthusiast and the interested consumer:

---

The hobbyist/enthusiast
- They are already keenly interested in what you have to offer.
- They actively want to know about your products and services.
- They are willing to accept a lot of copy – often, the more, the better (so long as it is lively, readable and relevant, and in a clear and logical order).
- They welcome your mailing and are happy to read your advert. They will make a point of picking up your leaflets.

---

> The interested consumer
> * They are in the market for what you are offering.
> * They want the facts/details so they can easily compare you with others.
> * They might feel overwhelmed by choice and information.
> * If it is a major purchase they might feel worried about making the wrong choice. They seek intelligent reassurance.
> * They welcome your information and want to know more.

You should see from the above examples how important it is to consider your audience and their needs. It makes your task easier because you have a good idea of what your reader wants and of what you should avoid. Were you to write copy suitable for an enthusiast, but aimed at busy managers, you would be onto a loser from the outset. For the busy owner of a smallish business you might write:

> ✔
> Dear Ms Lewis,
>
> **Halve your office heating bills**
>
> I know you're busy so I'll get straight to the point. I can cut your heating bill by 50%. Here's how …

This no-nonsense, straight-to-the-point approach works. A more ponderous letter (such as the example below) would end up in the 'wicker filing cabinet': the bin!

> ✘
> Dear Ms Lewis,
>
> I am writing to tell you about an amazing new concept in office insulation brought direct to this country from the US by Jacksonsville, the UK's premier ISO9000-accredited provider of insulation systems …

No busy person will struggle with such a letter to extract the relevant facts. They will give up. Even someone with an interest would have to labour to work out what you were getting at. So remember who you are writing for and what their needs are. Write for them, not for you.

Having considered *who* you are writing for, it is now time to turn your attention to *why* you are writing.

## Establishing your purpose

You should never produce marketing material for the sake of it. That sounds obvious, but you would be surprised how much material is produced by companies who have never considered why they are producing it and what they hope to achieve as a result. In my work I am frequently called in by clients to produce a brochure or a leaflet for them. When I ask the obvious question: 'Why do you want a leaflet?' they are at a loss to explain. It is something they have not thought about. They think they need a leaflet but they don't know why. As a copywriter, you cannot begin to write any marketing material until you have an answer to the question: why? Establish the purpose of the material you are writing. Let's say you are asked to write a new leaflet. Its purpose might be:

- To persuade or
- To inform or
- To sell or
- To educate or
- To build an image

A leaflet aimed at informing will contain lots of facts and information. One designed to build an image would be totally different. That's why it is so important to know the aim: without it you cannot choose the right content, or the appropriate words to convey the message.

Be clear on the purpose of your material. Let's say its aim is to sell. What are you selling? An image? A particular product or range of products? A service?

What action do you want readers to take as a result of reading what you have written? Do you want them to:

- Phone for further information?
- Complete and return a coupon?
- Visit one of your outlets?
- Ask for a quotation?
- Request a catalogue?
- Place an order?
- Make a donation?
- Take out a membership?

## Tone/personality

When we speak, it is clear to the listener what our tone is. We can say the same words but come across very differently depending on how we say them. For example, we can say the word 'hurry' in an angry or impatient way, in an imploring way, or in a questioning way. Visual clues such as facial expressions and body language reinforce our message. The written word is one-dimensional in comparison. All our meaning must be conveyed in words, without the added help of intonation or non-verbal clues. You need to decide on tone before you begin writing. Do you want to come across as friendly and informal? Authoritative? Caring?

By now you will have thought about who you are writing for and what their needs are. You will be clear on the purpose of your material and the intended outcome. You will also have decided on what tone to adopt. Finally it is time to consider the message.

## The message

This is perhaps the most important part of your planning. If you have a powerful message, you will find it easier to write powerful and persuasive copy. Your message (or messages) will be based on:

- Benefits
- USP
- Psychology – the reward for buying the product (beauty, cleaner washing) and possibly the 'fear factor': what will happen if you do not buy the product
- Proposition/offer

*Benefits*

Dull and lifeless copy promotes features. Readers are not interested in features, they want to know about benefits. What's the difference? Well, if you were to promote *features*, you might write:

> ✗ This craftsman-made sofa has dovetail joints, reinforced with metal rivets driven deep into the sofa's structure, giving it a rigid construction. Additionally the upholstery is double-Scotchsafe coated.

That focuses on the features of a product, such as the way it is made. A product's features are often of considerable interest to the company producing or selling an item. They may have put great effort into their development, and feel proud of what they have achieved. But their interest is not shared by the punter. Customers have no interest in features, only in the *benefits* of these features. For example:

> ✔ This craftsman-made sofa is so strong it will outlive you. Its tough, invisible protective coating will guard against all stains and spills, keeping your sofa as fresh as the day you bought it and dispensing with the need for expensive shampooing and dry cleaning.

In this example the benefits are clearly spelt out. The feature – dovetail joints reinforced with metal rivets – is presented as a benefit: the sofa is so strong it will outlive you. The double-Scotchsafe coated feature is explained as a benefit: no stains and no expensive shampooing. Don't be a feature-freak. Promote the benefits. If you find it easier, list the features first and then turn them into benefits. For example:

An office chair

| Features | Benefits |
| --- | --- |
| Ergonomic design | Won't give you back-ache |
| Fully adjustable | Will be comfortable whatever your height or build |
| Aluminium frame | Lightweight and easy to move |

## USP

This acronym stands for 'unique selling point' (sometimes also referred to as unique selling proposition). Your USP is the thing that makes your product or service unique – but remember that a USP is valid only if it is meaningful to your customers. Having a performance-enhancing piece of machinery is not a USP in its own right, it is merely a means to it. The USP arising from that might be that you can offer a faster service, dispatching an order in 12 hours, unlike the 48 hours offered by your rivals. You might base your USP on being:

- The oldest or newest
- The largest or smallest/most personal
- The best on price
- The best selling
- The first
- The most advanced
- The only provider of that particular service or product
- Able to offer special extras – e.g. a regular customer newsletter containing special offers, a free extended warranty, invitations to pre-sale previews, corporate hospitality

*Psychology: fear and rewards*

Good copy should in part work at a psychological level, persuading and influencing. It should indicate the reward of buying the product, presenting it in a way designed to appeal to feelings and emotion rather than logic. So you might suggest that a new mascara offers beauty and sophistication, not just thicker lashes. In the same way a car might be promoted not as offering a vehicle that will get you from A to B, but as freedom.

Copy should be positive, not negative: text that dwells heavily on what will happen if the customer does not buy can be counter-productive. Having said that, there are benefits in subtly hinting that buyers can avoid something unpleasant with this product, thereby fostering the fear factor at a subconscious level. You might suggest that the reader will be unfashionable, mean, uncaring, smelly ... or whatever, if they do not take up your offer. Of course, a blatant statement to this effect is inadvisable; it would offend and annoy your reader. Here's an example. Suppose you sell educational books. A promotion that claimed:

> ✗ If you turn down this offer your children's education will suffer. They will fall behind at school and never catch up. You will ensure your children are destined to a life of failure.

would cause an uproar. You need to be more subtle.

> ✔ Every parent wants the best for their children. Give yours a head start with our educational books. They will set your children up for a life of learning.

The message is the same: failure to take up the offer will result in parents giving their children a poorer start in life. But the second version presents it much more palatably and persuasively. Here's another example, this time a real-life advert for panty liners:

> [photo of a woman with the headline:]
> How do I stay fresh, clean and comfortable all day, every day?

The inference is that without these panty liners the woman would be dirty and uncomfortable. This device enables you to say something in an oblique way that would, if stated up-front, be rejected by the reader as nonsense or as downright insulting.

At this planning stage, all you need to do is identify what the fear factor is. Later on you can explore how this can be worked into your copy.

*Your proposition/offer*

This is the bottom line – it is what you are offering. It will comprise some or all of the following:

- Your product or service (mentioning benefits, USP, etc.)
- Any special offers, discounts or free gifts
- Payment options

## Writing the brief

If you work through each of the above stages you will end up with a clear brief for your writing assignment. It is always easier to write to a brief because you know who you are writing for, what they want to know, what key points you need to get across, and what effect you want to produce. Without a brief you are writing blindfold. To produce a brief for your next assignment, just complete the following:

> **THE BRIEF**
>
> **Assignment:**
>
> **Audience(s):**
>
> **Audience needs:**
>
> **Purpose of copy:**
>
> **Desired response/outcome:**

**Tone:**

**Benefits:**

**USP:**

**Psychology:**
**Rewards**
**Fear**

**Proposition/offer:**

Here's a completed brief, to illustrate how you might complete each section.

**Assignment:** Zoo leaflet

**Audience(s):** Parents with young children, living within 90 minutes' drive of the zoo

**Audience needs:** Bright and attractive, easy to digest information, and all the relevant details – opening hours; what there is to see; practical information such as nappy change, catering, etc.

**Purpose of copy:** (a) To persuade the reader that the zoo offers a fun and value-for-money day out for the whole family, (b) to inform them of the zoo's many attractions

**Desired response/outcome:** To get the reader to organize a family day out at the zoo

**Tone:** Friendly and fun

**Benefits:**
● It's a cheap day out: the entrance fee covers all activities (pony rides, face painting, etc.)
● There is more than enough to fill a whole day
● There's fun for the whole family: attractions for all ages include play areas for toddlers, ecology centre and global warming exhibition for teenagers, restaurant and wildlife cinema for adults
● It is a stress-free place for parents: the family-friendly environment features nappy-change facilities, children's menus, high chairs, etc.

**USP:**
● It is the only zoo to have a permanent ecology centre and wildlife cinema
● It is the only zoo with baby tigers
● It is the only zoo within a 100-mile radius

**Psychology:**
**Rewards**
Introducing children to the world's animals and to important issues such as ecology and global warming. Giving them an educational trip that is also highly enjoyable and memorable.
**Fear**
If you do not take your family to this zoo you will be neglecting their education and failing to equip them with the skills they will need as the future custodians of our planet.

**Proposition/offer:**
A value-for-money fun day out for the whole family. A family ticket costing just £15 allows two adults and up to four children in, making it one of the best and cheapest days out around.

Your brief acts as your personal checklist. When finally you complete the text for your marketing assignment, go back and look at your brief. Have you written in an appropriate style for the audience? Will readers take the necessary action? Have you conveyed the key messages? If you have missed anything, revise your copy. Try out your material on a few people. See if they can tell who it has been written for, what its purpose is, and what the reader should do after reading it.

# 3  Getting started

To get the perfect piece of copy, you need to know how to approach that blank sheet of paper. This chapter shows how to plan and shape a piece of writing, how to dump down ideas, and organize and group them. Then on to the actual writing. Find out how to revise your work, test it out on others, cut or rewrite text, and deal with the dreaded writer's block.

Many people find that getting started is the hardest part of writing. Once you're in full flow it's fine, but getting those first few sentences down can be hell. If you've done that all-important planning (covered in the previous chapter) you will find your task easier – though probably far from simple. Essentially there are six stages to writing copy:

- *Collecting/dumping* – jotting down your thoughts and ideas
- *Grouping* – putting your ideas into clear themes
- *Ordering* – putting your themes into a logical order
- *Placing* – deciding what is going where and how much space it should have
- *Writing* – doing a first draft
- *Revising* – working on subsequent drafts and polishing your finished work

## Collecting

Stage one in the writing process is the gathering of your ideas. Get a piece of paper and write down all your relevant thoughts, ideas and information in note form. 'Dump' down anything at all – in any order. If you don't complete this stage, you may find that you are so busy trying to remember all the thoughts and ideas zipping around in your head that you are unable to concentrate on the task of writing. There's also the risk that you will overlook something important. So don't skip this stage: it is important. Here's an example of what you might come up with during the collection process.

> **STRIDE: HI-STAR'S RUNNING SHOE**
> Product name – Stride
> Professional – used by Olympic runners
> Benefits

> Enhances running performance
> Comfortable
> Colours
> Guards against injury
> Materials
> Photos of the shoe
> Sports star endorsement? Roger Bannister? Top trainer? Olympic gold medallist?
> Order form
> Sizes
> Quality
> Construction of shoe

By collecting and dumping you will end up with a jumble of thoughts and ideas set out in no particular order. That's stage one completed: now for stage two, grouping.

## Grouping

Having compiled a list, read it through and group items into clear themes (adding any other ideas that spring to mind). Group related ideas. Add detail. Delete anything suspect or silly. You should end up with something like this:

> *Benefits*
> Grip-fast polyresin sole enhances running performance
> Double-thickness leather upper and ankle support guards against injury
> Contoured interior creates the most comfortable running shoe ever
>
> *Standard information*
> Price
> Order form
> Address
>
> *Product details*
> Sizes
> Colours
> Materials – leather uppers, polyresin sole
>
> *Illustrations*
> Fashion close-up shot of the shoe, perhaps in a running block
> Photo of the shoe in action – runner on track
> Computer-generated illustration of interior contours

Although you have not yet started to write, it's taking shape. You know what you want to say and who you want to say it to. You have the key points listed and clear groups/themes are emerging. Edit further at this stage if necessary.

## Ordering

Take your themes and put them into a clear and logical order. You can order things chronologically, alphabetically or in some other sequence. Whichever you go for, it must make sense to the reader, with each new theme or section leading on logically from the preceding one.

## Placing

This stage is not always necessary. It depends on what you are producing. Let's say you are writing a customer newsletter. So long as you know what your lead story is, what goes where on the inside pages may not matter too much. But with some marketing material, you need to be clear up-front about where things are going to go, and how much space each section will get. Take the example of the running shoe leaflet:

---

A4 sheet folded to A5

*Outer cover:* large photo of Roger Bannister holding the shoe. Short pithy quote. Logo
Quote and photo to have equal prominence in terms of design

*Inside page 1:* Introduction. Explain why Bannister is endorsing shoe. Bullet-point benefits

*Page 2:* Company credentials (half a page)
Practical info. – sizes, colours, order details

*Back page:* order form

---

By organizing the content logically and allocating each theme a slot, the writing task is easier. You can almost visualize the layout of the finished work as you begin to write.

## Writing

At last you are ready to start writing. Reread your brief (see Chapter 2) and look through any notes you have created during the ordering and placing stages of planning so that you are reminded of the task in hand. Now produce a first draft. Don't worry too much about style at this stage: it's only a draft and may end up being revised several times before you complete it. Going back to the running shoe example, your first draft might look something like this:

---

[outer cover]

'If the Stride had been around in my day, perhaps I'd be famous for the three-minute mile!'
[photo of Roger Bannister holding the shoe]
[caption] Sir Roger Bannister, the first runner to complete the four-minute mile

[Logo]

[page 1]
Why top runners choose the Stride

Roger Bannister is a running legend. Although well into retirement, he still runs every day. And the sports shoe he chooses is Hi-star's Stride. He's in good company. All the gold medallist runners in the last Olympics sported the Stride. Why? Because it's the best running shoe you can buy.

- **Enhance your running performance**
  The Stride features a unique grip-fast polyresin sole. It won't let you slip or slide, even in wet weather, so you can run sure and fast every time.
- **Guard against injury**
  A double-thickness leather upper, combined with ankle support, will help protect you from twists and sprains.
- **Protection from pain**
  Feel like you're running on air. The Stride has a contoured interior, making it the most comfortable running shoe ever. No more blisters or sore spots.

[page 2]
**Hi-star: Serving runners for decades**
Hi-star has been making running shoes for more than half a century. Stride, the best shoe we have ever made, is chosen by more professional runners than any other shoe. That shows how good it is.

**Great looks built to last**
- The Stride comes in a range of fashionable colours – mint green, crazy pink (only available up to size 8), yellow fizz, sea blue and, of course, black and white.

---

[show samples of the colours, each clearly labelled]

- We stock every size (including half sizes) from adult size 4 up to size 12.
- Supple, double-thickness leather uppers let your feet breathe, while offering protection and durability. The polyresin sole is hard wearing and helps cushion your feet, as does the natural cotton contoured insole. Each pair of Strides comes fitted with our unique no-fray laces.
- At only £39.95 we beat our competitors on price and performance.

Ordering is easy. Just complete the form overleaf and return it to us in the postage-paid envelope. Your shoes will arrive within a fortnight – guaranteed.

[back page]

## ORDER FORM

Yes! I want to order the shoes professional runners recommend. Please send me a pair of Hi-star Strides:

Name: .................................................................................

Address: ..............................................................................

Size: (from adult 4 up to 12, including half sizes) ......................

Colour: (remember Crazy Pink is available only up to size 8) ......

**Payment**

You can pay by cheque, debit or credit card.

I enclose a cheque for £.......... made payable to Hi-star.

Please charge my debit/credit card (delete as applicable)
Card number:
Expiry date:
Signature:

Return in the post-paid envelope, or post to Hi-star, Freepost LE15 113. Alternatively, debit and credit card orders can be faxed to us on 01123 245541.

Please tick here if you do **not** want to be sent details of other sports and running goods from top manufacturers ☐

After all that planning, a first draft can be something of a disappointment. But always remember that a first draft is an important starting point. It is extremely unlikely to be perfect; that's not the purpose of a draft, but of the finished piece. Also, remember that copy typed up onto A4 paper, devoid of design input, illustration and so on, always looks a little flat. Good design really helps bring your copy to life. So if your efforts look a bit lifeless at this stage, panic not. (Read Chapter 11 on copy and design working in harmony.)

## Revising

That's the first draft done. As I have said, don't expect to be able to get away with just one draft. You are likely to have to revise your work several times. Put your copy to one side and return to it later, preferably after a few days. You will find it easier to spot any stilted text, any inappropriate words or sections, any repetition. Reread what you have written through the eyes of the intended audience. Check that the style is right for your reader. Ensure your purpose is clear and that the necessary messages are conveyed. Mark any text you are not happy with. In particular look out for:

- Repetition – over-use of the same words or phrases
- Clichés – these should be avoided (unless you are using them in a witty way, for example: 'Now there's no need to cry over spilt milk' [an advert for a stain-resistant carpet] or 'The best thing since sliced bread' [an advert for an upmarket uncut loaf])
- Anything irrelevant
- Redundant words, e.g. *advance* planning (planning is always done in advance); *work* colleagues (colleagues are people you work with); 6 am *in the morning* (it is impossible for 6 am to be in the evening)
- Ambiguity
- Lack of clarity
- Consistency – for example, if you hyphenate the word 'co-ordinate' in the first paragraph, do so throughout
- Long screeds of unbroken text
- Omissions – is anything vital missing?
- Jargon
- Aptness of language – do your chosen words convey your intended meaning?
- Is there enough variety in sentence length?
- Can anything be pruned to aid brevity?

Having spotted the errors in your first draft, correct them. Rewrite any sections that need changing. Looking back at the above running-shoe example, you might decide on rereading that the Hi-star credentials bit was unnecessary. You've been in business for over 50 years, top runners already wear your shoes, so do you really need this section? By rereading your work after an acceptable interval, you are a little more objective and critical – and a great deal more refreshed.

Once you have completed as many revisions as necessary, it's time for a test drive. Try out your work on others. Don't pick your mother or your best friend: they will tell you your work is wonderful! If possible, select two or three people from the audience at which your writing is aimed. Listen carefully to the comments of your test-readers. If they don't understand something, find it boring, ill-organized or confusing, discuss with them what they would like to see. Take on board what you feel is reasonable.

## Starting over

But what if you hate the end product? The only thing to do is to start all over again. The more you write, the less often this will happen. Before you restart, look at your copy and analyse it. What bits do you like? Are there particular words, phrases or sections that you are pleased with? If so, retain them and see if they can be re-used. What is it that you dislike? Try to avoid this in the next draft. Never be afraid to bin your work. It is pointless struggling to make something of work that is meritless. Often a fresh start is easier (and the end-product better) than a rehash.

## Another method

The method of getting started discussed above is a clear and logical way to approach copywriting. It is a really useful one for those new to it or anyone who finds getting started really painful. Having said that, it's not the one I use. You might like to try both methods, to see which suits you best.

I start with one or more ideas. I write these down, which in turn spark others. I might perhaps start with an opening paragraph for a sales brochure. Half-way through it I could come up with another idea, thereby abandoning my initial effort. Ten minutes later I might have two opening paragraphs, a few buzzwords that I would like to include, a couple of good phrases, a closing paragraph, and an order form. After staring vacantly into space it suddenly becomes clear. I know more or less what I want to write and in what order. I'm not sure where it comes from or what the mental process is, but if it works, who am I to question it?

So that's how I begin. Sadly, for all of us there are times when getting started is just about the hardest thing facing us. The more we think about it, the harder it gets. Indeed, it can be so hard as to be impossible. The popular term for this affliction is 'writer's block'.

## Remedies for writer's block

Even the most seasoned copywriters sometimes suffer from writer's block. Publisher-turned-author Michael Legat has written widely on how to write and get published. He says of writer's block, in his book *Writing For Pleasure and Profit*: 'I have little sympathy ... writer's block has become a fashionable ailment, and it is certainly easier and more impressive to say that you are affected with it than that you are lazy.' There is some truth in this, but I don't entirely share Legat's rather harsh view (having acutely suffered this condition several times during the writing of this book!).

We've all been there. You sit at your word processor, gazing at the blank screen. Somehow the words just don't come. No inspiration can be found. Anything you do manage to write is rubbish. Depression sets in. Your mind begins to wander. You contemplate what to wear for Jamie's party, or what to cook when the Dibdens come to dinner. Efforts to focus on the task at hand are futile.

When writer's block sets in as hard as concrete, no good will come of forcing yourself to remain at your desk. But don't panic. There are various techniques for getting started again when writer's block strikes:

---

**TWENTY-ONE TIPS FOR UNBLOCKING YOUR MIND**

● **Dumping rubbish**
My own method is to write anything at all, even if it is complete trash, until the words begin to flow again.

● **Different assignment**
Try switching topic to see if it helps. You could even write about your writer's block!

● **Basic needs**
If you are hungry or tired, you will not be at your best. If you feel shattered, put off your writing to another day (if that's possible). If you must press on, then at least rest your head on your desk, with your eyes closed, for 15 minutes. It will help. As for hunger, that's obvious. Get something to eat. You will feel much better afterwards.

● **Start easy**
Start writing the easy bit of your copy – an order form, contact

---

details, anything. At least you are achieving something. You might find that you are able to tackle a slightly harder bit of text, and so on. Eventually you are back in full swing – or so the theory goes!

- **A wee dram**
Some writers swear that alcohol oils their creativity. I know of others who blame alcohol for ruining their careers. If you are working at home, perhaps a glass of wine will help you get started, though it might raise a few eyebrows in the office.

- **Forget style**
Write what you can, however dreadful. You can go back later and polish it. The important thing is to start writing. Once you've got it on paper, at least you are in a position to edit or redraft.

- **Coffee and cake**
If you've been trying and trying without success, take a break. Nip out for coffee and cake, and mull over your writing assignment. In the more relaxed atmosphere of a café you might find that the elusive idea on which your copy will be based comes to you – assuming your boss doesn't mind you leaving your desk!

- **Dictate it**
Try saying what you want to write. Talk to a tape recorder, or talk to a real person. You are less likely to be lost for words when speaking than writing. Having to talk out loud can help you to get going.

- **Get physical**
Adrenaline is a product of physical exercise. Go for a bracing walk or a quick jog round the block, then use the resultant adrenaline surge to recharge your brain.

- **A change of activity**
If you're getting nowhere with your writing, try doing something else for a while. Make a few phone calls, catch up on some reading, go through your in-tray. After a reasonable interval, get back to your writing.

- **Schedule an a.m. session**
Apparently one's brain is at its best in the morning (though I'm sure that mine is sharper in the evening). If you find it difficult to get down to writing, try to do it first thing, while you are fresh and your brain is in prime form. Experts suggest that you take a short (perhaps five-minute) break after 45 minutes, to restore concentration.

- **Avoid mid-afternoon writing**
Mental decline appears to set into most 'nine to fivers' at

about 4 pm. Attempting to start writing then is likely to be harder, with writer's block far more likely. So avoid this slot if you can.

- **Have a mental warm-up**

  Try warming up your brain. Play a few word games, do a crossword, or have a go at some of the exercises in Chapter 10.

- **Reach for inspiration**

  Look at other people's adverts, brochures, leaflets and newsletters. See if you can find inspiration from the work of others whom you admire.

- **Share it with others**

  Writing is a solitary business. If you're getting nowhere fast, go and talk it over with colleagues. See if they can provide you with a different insight, a new angle or an enlightened thought.

- **Have a brainstorm**

  Jot down anything you can related to what you are writing about – quotes, key words, adjectives. See if any of these helps you get started.

- **A bit of discipline**

  Writer's block is simply the result of laziness or lack of application, or so some believe. Sometimes you will just have to force yourself to get on with it. Quit the delaying tactics (tidying your desk, making a cup of tea), admit that you are being lazy, then settle down to work. Your writing assignment will not go away, so you've no choice but to knuckle down. Get everything you need (paper, refreshments, notes, etc.) so that you have no excuse for leaving your desk. Such excuses merely break your concentration and make it even harder to get down to it.

- **More understanding**

  Often there is a deep-seated reason why some people suffer from chronic writer's block. It may be to do with fear of failure. Try to analyse why you find writing so hard, then do something about it.

Like most people I find it difficult to motivate myself when working on a dull or boring assignment. Although copywriting can be very satisfying, like all jobs there's a downside. Not everything you are asked to write will fill you with enthusiasm and leave you raring to go. Much 'bread and butter' copywriting can be dreary; the more of it you have to do, the more depressing it is. So when your heart sinks at the prospect of yet another straightforward and unchallenging project, take heart.

It is normal for you to feel this way. So put your despair to one side, adopt an ultra-professional attitude, knuckle down and get the job completed to your usual high standards.

● **Reward yourself**
Give yourself a small treat for every page you write, or every hour you work. As a chocoholic I opt for a Rolo every hour.

● **Add some pressure**
Put yourself under a little pressure. Set a deadline for the finished product and stick to it. Decide when you are going to do your writing, put it in your diary and block off the time.

● **Real deadline magic**
If none of the above remedies works, an impending deadline will get you moving again. If you've got to do it, somehow you will. And as I have already said, the more you do it, the easier it gets.

# 4 Nine routes to punchier copy

This chapter looks at simple but effective ways to ensure your copy packs a punch. Find out how to use plain English effectively. Learn how to paint vivid pictures using words. Discover the ABC of good copywriting and pick up tips on how to break up your copy into bite-size chunks.

So far we have looked at the technical side of copywriting – researching, planning, drafting and redrafting. If you follow the advice in the previous chapters you will be able to write, but will you be able to do it with flair? Only if you know what turns competent writing into powerful prose. That's what I will explore in this chapter: turning well-planned words into sizzling copy.

You can spot the work of a good professional copywriter in an instant. It stands out, it demands to be read, it is sharp and snappy. What do the pros do to give their work these qualities? There are nine techniques they use to ensure their work has dimension and bite. The techniques are so simple that you can pick them up and start using them immediately, instantly improving the impact of your copy.

## 1 The first person

The easiest way to make any marketing material more lively is to use the first person. It will instantly give your copy a lift. You can always tell an inexperienced copywriter because they tend to write in the third person. They might write:

> ✗ The Spingate Shopping Centre offers customers top name shops, free parking and a free shuttle bus from the town centre. Shoppers will find that the Spingate provides everything the High Street can, and more besides.

The third person makes copy impersonal, remote and distant, so use the first person as much as you can. It's much more intimate, more one-to-one, more direct – as you can see from this example:

> ✔ At the Spingate Shopping Centre you'll find top name shops, free parking and a free shuttle bus from the town centre. We provide everything the High Street can, and more besides.

Don't be afraid to use 'we' and 'you'. It's so much better than talking about abstractions like 'the customer', 'the viewer' and 'the purchaser'. When talking to a real, living, breathing person, don't dehumanize them by using the third person. You would never do it face to face. I've used the first person throughout this book, enabling me to talk direct to you. Start talking direct to your readers.

## 2 Showing, not telling

The real hallmark of good copy is text that shows, not tells. If you ever attend a short story or novel-writing class, one of the first tips you will pick up is 'show, don't tell'. Don't give a pedestrian account of what is happening, show it happening through your use of lively, active and descriptive language. Take the reader with you, make them feel involved, part of the action and not just a spectator. When it comes to copywriting, the same rule applies: show, don't tell. You can show visually, by using a photograph, or you can show by painting a picture with words.

Here's an example of telling:

> ✗ Slimline 100 is a simple, inexpensive and revolutionary weight loss programme that can help you lose pounds fast. It has helped many users achieve dramatic weight loss with little effort or willpower.

As a piece of writing it is fine. It states the facts clearly and persuasively, but it fails to conjure up a real picture that involves the reader. It is just telling. Here's how you show it:

> ✔ Last year Mary was 18 stone. Now she's a slinky size 10. You can achieve the same dramatic weight loss with Slimline 100. Picture yourself turning heads in skin-tight dresses, short skirts, skimpy bikinis. With Slimline 100 it need not be just a dream.

By showing, you are not just listing what the product can do, you are demonstrating it in a powerful and personal way. You are involving the reader, offering them a taste of what the product can do for them. Much marketing material offers the opportunity to reinforce with photographs the picture you paint with words. When Oprah Winfrey lost nearly five stones, she demonstrated the enormity of her weight loss by showing a supermarket trolley laden with 67 lb of lard. That's a brilliant illustration of how it is better to show than tell. Supermarket chain Sainsbury's used the same trick to show the superiority of their Reward Card. Full-page newspaper adverts showed two photographs. One was a supermarket trolley piled high with scores of jars of coffee. It was captioned 'To get 300 points with the other supermarkets' cards'. The second photo showed a super-market trolley with just three jars of coffee in it, captioned: 'To get 300 points with your Sainsbury's Reward Card.'

This rule can be applied in so many ways. Don't just tell the benefits of loft conversion (more space, for example, or added value to your home), show the end-result (an extra bedroom and en-suite bathroom). Don't rely on photos to do all the showing, use words too.

## 3 Appropriate abbreviations

Another way to give vitality to your writing is to mimic the spoken word, which you can achieve by abbreviation. Never be afraid to abbreviate where appropriate – 'I've' instead of 'I have', for example. A few people regard such contractions as unacceptable in written English. Let them. Most of us prefer to read copy that flows, and appropriate abbreviations do aid flow, making text much more chatty, informal, friendly and readable. You will see that I have used this technique to give this book a less stuffy feel.

This advice is probably at odds with what you had drummed into you at school. So what? Copywriting is not the same as writing an essay or a school project. Creative copywriting breaks the rules. What might offend the grammatical purists may be perfect fodder for copywriters. So don't feel too bound by what Miss English-Teacher told you. Be led by what feels and sounds right. Many of the strictures of English usage are getting more relaxed. Indeed the new *Chambers Dictionary* (published in 1996) says that splitting infinitives is quite acceptable.

## 4 Situational copy

Sometimes copy takes on more meaning if you can link it to where it is being heard or read. For example, imagine you have just tucked into a slap-up meal. You've paid the bill and the waitress hands you your receipt. You find the following printed on it:

> ✔ We hope you enjoyed your meal. In the time it took you to eat it, 900 children died of starvation in the Third World. The cost of your meal would be enough to feed all of them. Please make a donation to War on Famine.

You'd have to be a hard person not to feel a pang of guilt about your own wealth and privilege compared with Third World children's. The above approach links a specific (the meal you have just eaten) with another specific (the 900 children who have just died). It is far more powerful than this:

> ✗ 900 children die of starvation every hour. Just £25 could feed all of them for a day. Please make a donation to War on Famine.

The second example does not connect with your immediate experience – the slap-up meal. It is far too general and far easier to ignore.

This following real-life example (from an advert on the London Underground) illustrates the same point, albeit in a less extreme way:

> Victoria Line trains will be running frequently today. Without Nurofen Cold and Flu alas so will your nose

The copy is appropriate to the situation of the adverts on the Underground. So is this (for headache powders, displayed inside a bus):

> Just the ticket for a headache

It's not startlingly clever, but it still links to the situation. People reading it will be clutching their bus tickets, so the link exists, however tenuously. The same product is also advertised on bus exteriors:

> Gets to work faster than this bus

On a similar line, a fast-food chain was running an advertising campaign using the slogan 'You got it!'. On their bus ads they ran:

> Wanna catch this bus? You got it!

## 5 Writing that follows the ABC

Look at any piece of good copy – brochures, leaflets, adverts, anything at all -- and you will see that it adheres to the ABC of copywriting:

*A is for:*

*Accurate* – everything you write must be accurate. Check all spelling, all phone numbers, addresses, prices and other details. There must be no typos. Everything should be checked and double-checked for accuracy.

*Appropriate* – ensure that the language (and design) you use is appropriate for the intended audience. A four-letter word in the company of 'the lads down the boozer' may not raise an eyebrow, but the same word at a WI coffee morning would cause horror and disgust. It's the same with copy. Choose words carefully. Hip buzzwords will cause blank looks in a leaflet aimed at pensioners!

*Ambiguity* – avoid ambiguity. Everything should have one meaning and one meaning alone (unless you are deliberately using puns and *doubles-entendre*).

*B is for:*

*Brief* – it is harder to be brief than verbose, but your aim must always be to be as brief as possible. Anything longer than necessary is just padding. Look for sloppy writing you can tighten up. So, instead of writing: 'we are the only company to offer you ...', say: 'only Bergen's offer you ...'. Don't write: 'all the features you will ever need', say: 'every feature you'll ever need'.

*Bright* – your writing should shine. It should have light and life.

*C is for:*

*Clear* – every sentence should be clear and easily understood. Readers should not have to reread to garner your meaning.

*Consistent* – ensure spelling etc. is consistent throughout.

## 6 Good use of euphemisms

Sometimes marketing copy requires tact. Let's say you are selling clothing for fat people. You might find yourself describing your customers as having a 'fuller figure'. Or calling your cheap hotel 'budget-priced'. These euphemisms are important. People know that 'affordable' really means 'cheap', but calling a spade a spade can be counter-productive if it forces your customers to acknowledge an unpalatable truth: that they are fat or broke. Make them feel good about the purchase, not miserable.

## 7 Words with a personality

It is easy when you listen to someone speaking to get a feel for their personality. A chat with someone will leave you feeling that they are bubbly, shy, businesslike, friendly ... or whatever. You can also get an insight into personality through someone's writing. You should be able to spot writers who are grovelling, arrogant, lacking in confidence, slimeballs, helpful – or a hundred other personality types. It will come across in their choice of words. As a copywriter you need to learn how to be a split personality, taking on different personalities according to the writing assignment. Decide what personality you want to convey. Helpful and knowledgeable? Down-to-earth? Knowing how you want to come across will help you write in the appropriate style.

## 8 Plain English

The best copy is written in plain English. Pick up any tabloid newspaper and you will see that while the content might not be to your taste, the copy is eminently readable. You can spring through it with ease. There's no stumbling on difficult words, no grappling with long and complex paragraphs. It's an easy read. Your copy should be too – however upmarket it is.

You don't have to adopt a tabloid style to produce copy that is easy to tackle for the reader, but you do have to steer clear of jargon and write in a down-to-earth, accessible way. Remember that jargon is like a foreign language. There's no point in talking to someone in Italian if they only understand French. Of course, it can be perfectly legitimate and extremely useful to use jargon – if understood by both writer and reader. But as a general rule, try not to be a jargonaut.

The *Hutchinson Concise Dictionary of English Usage* says of plain English: 'Plain English is clear, concise, effective, interesting English. It saves time, paper, and misunderstanding, and so it saves money ... Research shows that simple language sells products and services better than any other kind.' To me these are powerful reasons why marketing copywriters should adopt plain English as their language.

Plain English is characterized by:

- Short words
- Fairly short sentences (15–20 words)
- No jargon or unnecessary technical terms
- No legalese or officialese
- No padding or puffery
- Use of the first person
- A clear and logical order
- An understanding of what the reader needs to know

If you would like to know more about plain English, there are a couple of organizations you should get in touch with. The first is the Plain English Campaign (PO Box 3, New Mills, Stockport, SK12 4QP. Tel. 01663 734541). They produce an *A–Z Guide of Alternative*

*Words* and a pack on how to write letters in plain English, and they run courses. They also operate the 'Crystal Mark', a symbol you can display on your material (subject to approval by the Campaign, and payment of the appropriate fee) as a sign that your writing is clear and gobbledegook-free.

You should also get in touch with the Plain Language Commission (The Castle, 29 Stoneheads, Whaley Bridge, Stockport, SK12 7BB. Tel. 01663 733177) which was set up by Martin Cutts, the co-founder of the Plain English Campaign. They can advise on the readability of copy and offer advice to ensure your design aids clarity. The Plain Language Commission, too, offers a 'kitemark', the 'Clear English Standard'. It works in a similar way to the Plain English Campaign, although it costs less. You might also like to get hold of a copy of Martin Cutt's *The Plain English Guide* (£4.99, Oxford).

The Plain English Commission have produced a Plain English Code (reproduced here with permission). Although it is written for officials, it contains much good advice for copywriters. Why not sign up to it now?

---

Name: .................................... Date: ....................................

I will

- Match my writing to the needs and knowledge of the readers, remembering that many of them will be baffled by official jargon and procedures.
- Consider carefully the purpose and message before starting to write, remembering that clear writing and clear thinking go hand in hand.
- Structure the document clearly, perhaps with lists, headings and a pithy summary of key points.
- Write sentences which average 15–20 words.
- Keep the word order simple by putting the doer early in the sentence and following it with an active voice verb.
- Take pride in everyday English, sound grammar and accurate punctuation.
- Use 'I', 'we' and 'you' to make the writing more human.
- Maintain the flow by starting some sentences with link words like 'but', 'however', 'so' and 'because'.
- Use commands when writing instructions.
- Cut verbiage.
- Tell customers and colleagues clearly, concisely and courteously what has happened, how the situation stands, and what they can expect next.
- Test high-use documents with typical users.

---

## 9 Bite-sized chunks of copy

There is nothing worse in marketing copy than acres of unbroken text: it is a guaranteed turn-off for readers. It overwhelms, daunts, hurts one's eyes and fills the poor reader with dread. The mere sight of all this text is enough to deter many from even attempting to read it. Interestingly, what matters is not how long your copy is, but how long your reader *thinks* it is. One page of unbroken copy is more difficult to read than two pages of bite-size chunks. There are various tricks for converting long screeds of text into readable and easily digestible chunks.

*Bullet points*

My favourite device is the humble old bullet point. It offers a wonderfully simple yet effective way of presenting what would otherwise be rather daunting lists. Instead of writing:

> ✗ Every hotel in the Heritage chain offers: an indoor heated swimming pool, jacuzzi and sauna; fully equipped gym; plush rooms with satellite TV, minibar and trouser press; a bar and restaurant; business facilities and secretarial services; mini-cinema; free parking and free shuttle bus to the nearest airport.

try bullet points instead:

> ✔ Every hotel in the Heritage chain offers:
> - An indoor heated swimming pool, jacuzzi and sauna
> - Fully equipped gym
> - Plush rooms with satellite TV, minibar and trouser press
> - A bar and restaurant
> - Business facilities and secretarial services
> - Mini-cinema
> - Free parking and free shuttle bus to the nearest airport

The bullet-pointed list is clearer, less overwhelming, and it gives each of the items in the list more prominence.

*Callouts/pull quotes*

A callout, sometimes known as a pull quote, is a useful device both for breaking up text and for drawing attention to a particularly important section of copy. Here's an example:

---

**GARAVELLI'S: BRINGING THE MEDITERRANEAN TO BRITAIN**

Garavelli's terracotta pots are hand-made in the traditional way in a string of picturesque Tuscan villages. Each pot is individually thrown, shaped and decorated, then fired at high temperatures to make it frost-proof, essential for our chillier climes. No two pots are the same, unlike the mass produced pots available in garden centres. Every Garavelli pot has its own personality and each bears the signature of the maker.

**Each pot is individually thrown, shaped and decorated, then fired at high temperatures to make it frost-proof, essential for our chillier climes.**

Bring the warmth and colour of Tuscany to your own garden with a Garavelli hand-crafted terracotta pot. Available only by mail order, direct from Garavelli's. Call for a brochure. Prices start at just £9.99 for a 12-inch pot.

---

The callout breaks up the text, while simultaneously highlighting a key section of copy. It is a technique that can be used in leaflets, brochures, adverts and newsletter articles.

*Boxes*

Sometimes you can break up a page of text by 'boxing off' a section of it. Rather like callouts, a box can both break up text and draw attention to the text selected for boxing. Below you can see a page from a newsletter featuring unbroken text. As you will see, it looks rather dense. Following that you will see the same text, but the use of boxes creates a more readable and lively page. So when you come to write long copy, look out for anything that can be boxed.

---

**INDIAN FOOD WITH A DIFFERENCE**

Vegetarians in Anyville can now enjoy gourmet Indian food, thanks to the opening of Rajah's, the town's latest restaurant. Although not exclusively vegetarian (it has a small selection of chicken and fish dishes), Rajah's has an extensive and impressive vegetarian menu, with a number of vegan dishes.

Rajah's is quite unlike other Indian restaurants. There's no flock wallpaper to be seen, no paper tablecloths or plastic flowers. The elegant decor includes handmade tiles specially commissioned in India, imported rosewood tables and chairs, original Indian art,

---

and handprinted table linen adorned with Rajah's distinctive Paisley logo.

The emphasis is on fine food prepared in a traditional manner. While Rajah's kitchen is brand new, many of the utensils are the same as those used in India hundreds of years ago. The chefs believe that the use of original cooking implements creates a more authentic taste and texture. Each dish leaving Rajah's kitchen is guaranteed to be free from colourings, additives and preservatives.

The owners of Rajah's made a 10,000-mile round trip to recruit its chefs, one from the north of India and the other from the south. They bring with them specialist knowledge of a wide range of regional dishes, such as the rich, sweetly spiced main courses from the south, featuring nuts, coconut milk and lemon, as well as the more familiar northern Indian food, such as matar panir, a dish made with peas and cubes of tofu-like home-made cottage cheese.

Vegetarians can choose from 11 starters, 20 main courses, seven side dishes, seven types of rice, and 11 types of bread. The first courses are impressively varied, ranging from Bhelpuris (a Bombay roadside snack of puffed rice, crushed potatoes and tamarind sauce) to Dal Vada, crispy dumplings made with crushed chick peas, yellow lentils and onions. You'll also find more familiar starters, such as samosa and pakora.

The main courses, too numerous to mention, are split into north Indian cuisine, south Indian dishes, and 'thalis'. A thali is a large plate, on which are assembled a number of smaller dishes, rather like a meze. There is a north and a south Indian thali, a special Rajah's thali, and a vegan one.

Anyone for pudding? Rajah's offers the usual range of desserts (kulfi, halwa and gulab jamun) as well as some unusual and mouth-watering concoctions, such as Shrikhand, a golden yoghurt dessert garnished with saffron and pistachio, or kheer, a pudding made with rice, nuts, raisins and saffron.

There are even Indian drinks. Lassi is a delicious yoghurt drink, and Rajah's serve it in several varieties, including mango flavour, namkeen lassi (salty and subtly spiced) and meethi lassi, which is sweet, smooth and thirst-quenching. There's also south Indian coffee on the menu, Indian tea, and herbal tea.

So if you fancy an Indian meal with a difference, try Rajah's. And if you're really lucky, you might choose a night when Indian classical musicians are performing.

## INDIAN FOOD WITH A DIFFERENCE

Vegetarians in Anyville can now enjoy gourmet Indian food, thanks to the opening of Rajah's, the town's latest restaurant. Although not exclusively vegetarian (it has a small selection of chicken and fish dishes), Rajah's has an extensive and impressive vegetarian menu, with a number of vegan dishes.

Rajah's is quite unlike other Indian restaurants. There's no flock wallpaper to be seen, no paper tablecloths or plastic flowers. The elegant decor includes handmade tiles specially commissioned in India, imported rosewood tables and chairs, original Indian art, and handprinted table linen adorned with Rajah's distinctive Paisley logo.

The emphasis is on fine food prepared in a traditional manner. While Rajah's kitchen is brand new, many of the utensils are the same as those used in India hundreds of years ago. The chefs believe that the use of original cooking implements creates a more authentic taste and texture. Each dish leaving Rajah's kitchen is guaranteed to be free from colourings, additives and preservatives.

### MORE CHOICE
Vegetarians can choose from:
- 11 starters
- 20 main courses
- seven side dishes
- seven types of rice
- 11 types of bread

### ANYONE FOR PUDDING?
Rajah's offers the usual range of desserts (kulfi, halwa and gulab jamun) as well as some unusual and mouth-watering concoctions, such as Shrikhand, a golden yoghurt dessert garnished with saffron and pistachio, or kheer, a pudding made with rice, nuts, raisins and saffron.

The owners of Rajah's made a 10,000-mile round trip to recruit its chefs, one from the north of India and the other from the south. They bring with them specialist knowledge of a wide range of regional dishes, such as the rich, sweetly spiced main courses from the south, featuring nuts, coconut milk and lemon, as well as the more familiar northern Indian food, such as matar panir, a dish made with peas and cubes of tofu-like home-made cottage cheese.

The first courses are impressively varied, ranging from Bhelpuris (a Bombay roadside snack of puffed rice, crushed potatoes and tamarind sauce) to Dal Vada, crispy dumplings made with crushed chick peas, yellow lentils and onions. You'll also find more familiar starters, such as samosa and pakova.

The main courses, too numerous to mention, are split into north Indian cuisine, south Indian dishes, and 'thalis'. A thali is a large plate, on which are assembled a number of smaller dishes, rather like a meze. There is a north and a south Indian thali, a special Rajah's thali, and a vegan one.

There are even Indian drinks. Lassi is a delicious yoghurt drink, and Rajah's serve it in several varieties, including mango flavour, namkeen lassi (salty and subtly spiced) and meethi lassi, which is sweet, smooth and thirst-quenching. There's also south Indian coffee on the menu, Indian tea, and herbal tea.

So if you fancy an Indian meal with a difference, try Rajah's. And if you're really lucky, you might choose a night when Indian classical musicians are performing.

*Subheadings*

This common device is surprisingly neglected. Simple subheadings can break up text, signpost the reader and entice them to read on (if you can come up with interesting subheads). Take the example of the Indian restaurant featured above. See how much better and more interesting it looks with subheadings:

### INDIAN FOOD WITH A DIFFERENCE

Vegetarians in Anyville can now enjoy gourmet Indian food, thanks to the opening of Rajah's, the town's latest restaurant. Although not exclusively vegetarian (it has a small selection of chicken and fish dishes), Rajah's has an extensive and impressive vegetarian menu, with a number of vegan dishes.

**No flock wallpaper!**

Rajah's is quite unlike other Indian restaurants. There's no flock wallpaper to be seen, no paper tablecloths or plastic flowers. The elegant decor includes handmade tiles specially commissioned in India, imported rosewood tables and chairs, original Indian art, and handprinted table linen adorned with Rajah's distinctive Paisley logo.

The emphasis is on fine food prepared in a traditional manner. While Rajah's kitchen is brand new, many of the utensils are the same as those used in India hundreds of years ago. The chefs believe that the use of original cooking implements creates a more authentic taste and texture. Each dish leaving Rajah's kitchen is guaranteed to be free from colourings, additives and preservatives.

### 10,000 mile trip to recruit chefs

The owners of Rajah's made a 10,000-mile round trip to recruit its chefs, one from the north of India and the other from the south. They bring with them specialist knowledge of a wide range of regional dishes, such as the rich, sweetly spiced main courses from the south, featuring nuts, coconut milk and lemon, as well as the more familiar northern Indian food, such as matar panir, a dish made with peas and cubes of tofu-like home-made cottage cheese.

### Bombay roadside snacks

Vegetarians can choose from 11 starters, 20 main courses, seven side dishes, seven types of rice, and 11 types of bread. The first courses are impressively varied, ranging from Bhelpuris (a Bombay roadside snack of puffed rice, crushed potatoes and tamarind sauce) to Dal Vada, crispy dumplings made with crushed chick peas, yellow lentils and onions. You'll also find more familiar starters, such as samosa and pakora.

The main courses, too numerous to mention, are split into north Indian cuisine, south Indian dishes, and 'thalis'. A thali is a large plate, on which are assembled a number of smaller dishes, rather like a meze. There is a north and a south Indian thali, a special Rajah's thali, and a vegan one.

Anyone for pudding? Rajah's offers the usual range of desserts (kulfi, halwa and gulab jamun) as well as some unusual and mouth-watering concoctions, such as Shrikhand, a golden yoghurt dessert garnished with saffron and pistachio, or kheer, a pudding made with rice, nuts, raisins and saffron.

### Indian classical music

There are even Indian drinks. Lassi is a delicious yoghurt drink, and Rajah's serve it in several varieties, including mango flavour, namkeen lassi (salty and subtly spiced) and meethi lassi, which is sweet, smooth and thirst-quenching. There's also south Indian coffee on the menu, Indian tea, and herbal tea.

So if you fancy an Indian meal with a difference, try Rajah's. And if you're really lucky, you might choose a night when Indian classical musicians are performing.

These techniques can combine to create copy that looks readable (half the battle!). Here's an example of the newsletter page employing all the copy-breaking devices. Compare it with the original version on page 39. I know which I'd rather read!

---

## INDIAN FOOD WITH A DIFFERENCE

Vegetarians in Anyville can now enjoy gourmet Indian food, thanks to the opening of Rajah's, the town's latest restaurant. Although not exclusively vegetarian (it has a small selection of chicken and fish dishes), Rajah's has an extensive and impressive vegetarian menu, with a number of vegan dishes.

**No flock wallpaper!**

Rajah's is quite unlike other Indian restaurants. There's no flock wallpaper to be seen, no paper tablecloths or plastic flowers. The elegant decor includes handmade tiles specially commissioned in India, imported rosewood tables and chairs, original Indian art, and handprinted table linen adorned with Rajah's distinctive Paisley logo.

> **While Rajah's kitchen is brand new, many of the utensils are the same as those used by Indians hundreds of years ago ... Each dish leaving Rajah's kitchen is guaranteed to be free from colourings, additives and preservatives.**

The emphasis is on fine food prepared in a traditional manner. While Rajah's kitchen is brand new, many of the utensils are the same as those used in India hundreds of years ago. The chefs believe that the use of original cooking implements creates a more authentic taste and texture. Each dish leaving Rajah's kitchen is guaranteed to be free from colourings, additives and preservatives.

**10,000 mile trip to recruit chefs**

The owners of Rajah's made a 10,000-mile round trip to recruit its chefs, one from the north of India and the other from the south. They bring with them specialist knowledge of a wide range of regional dishes, such as the rich, sweetly spiced main courses from the south, which feature nuts, coconut milk and lemon, as well as the more familiar northern Indian food, such as matar panir, a dish made with peas and cubes of tofu-like home-made cottage cheese.

**Bombay roadside snacks**

> **MORE CHOICE**
> Vegetarians can
> choose from:
> - 11 starters
> - 20 main courses
> - seven side dishes
> - seven types of rice
> - 11 types of bread

The first courses are impressively varied, ranging from Bhelpuris (a Bombay roadside snack of puffed rice, crushed potatoes and tamarind sauce) to Dal Vada, crispy dumplings made with crushed chick peas, yellow lentils and onions. You'll also find more familiar starters, such as samosa and pakora.

The main courses, too numerous to mention, are split into north Indian cuisine, south Indian dishes, and 'thalis'. A thali is a large plate, on which are assembled a number of smaller dishes, rather like a meze. There is a north and a south Indian thali, a special Rajah's thali, and a vegan one.

Anyone for pudding? Rajah's offers the usual range of desserts (kulfi, halwa and gulab jamun) as well as some unusual and mouth-watering concoctions, such as Shrikhand, a golden yoghurt dessert garnished with saffron and pistachio, or kheer, a pudding made with rice, nuts, raisins and saffron.

**Indian classical music**
There are even Indian drinks. Lassi is a delicious yoghurt drink, and Rajah's serve it in several varieties, including mango flavour, namkeen lassi (salty and subtly spiced) and meethi lassi, which is sweet, smooth and thirst-quenching. There's also south Indian coffee on the menu, Indian tea, and herbal tea.

So if you fancy an Indian meal with a difference, try Rajah's. And if you're really lucky, you might choose a night when Indian classical musicians are performing.

# 5 Grammar and English

If grammar fills you with fear, this chapter is for you. Discover the painless way to write grammatically. Learn how to restructure your sentences to make them more lively. Discover the most common grammatical mistakes and how to avoid them. Find out how to remove sexism and other bias from your writing.

The dreaded grammar! You'll be pleased to hear that this chapter does not go into the terrifying complexities of grammar. There's no need for screeds of complex grammatical rules here, because whether you know it or not, you will already have (by and large) an instinctive feel for correct grammar. As long as your grammar is correct, does it really matter whether you understand why it is right? 'So what?' if you don't know what a 'past participle' or a 'conjunction' are! What matters is that you know how to use them. We all know that 'I are no good at grammar, is I?' is ungrammatical, even though we might struggle to explain why.

Of course, it would be too much to hope that a book on writing could avoid the subject of grammar altogether. Correct grammar is essential for effective copy. Thankfully you probably adhere to most of the rules already. It's the common grammatical errors that we will concentrate on here. Let's start with the seven most common mistakes.

## Seven common grammatical mistakes

*1 Commas for full stops or colons*

So often I see commas where there should be full stops. If you make this mistake, your writing will be harder to understand. And remember, the harder it is to read and make sense of, the less likely it is to be read at all. Here's an example of what I mean. It's from a printed sign above the doorway of my local Pizza Hut:

> ✗ Welcome to Pizza Hut, please wait to be seated.

Here we have two completely discrete sentences, making two distinct points, separated by a comma. As we all know, sentences are separated by full stops. Here are some common examples from marketing material that make the same error:

> ✗ Place your order now, this offer expires at the end of the month.

This would be better as

> ✔ Place your order now, as this offer expires at the end of the month.

or

> ✔ Place your order now: this offer expires at the end of the month.

Another example:

> ✗ If you seek value look no further, we have plenty of offers to tempt you.

This should read:

> ✔ If you seek value, look no further. We have plenty of offers to tempt you.

When placing a comma, think: 'is a comma required here, or have I reached the end of the sentence?' Sometimes you might feel that a comma would be wrong, but a full stop would be too final. In such cases the colon is useful. As in this example:

> ✔ Place your order now: this offer expires at the end of the month.

### 2 Singulars for plurals

It is not uncommon for people to take a singular noun and add a plural verb. For example, you often see:

> ✗ there *are* a host of benefits attached to this deal ...

As host is singular, it should read:

> ✔ there *is* a host of ...

Another example:

> ✘ You'll be spoilt for choice, as there *are* plenty to choose from

should be:

> ✔ You'll be spoilt for choice, as there *is* plenty to choose from

Always check that your noun and verb agree.

### 3 Wrong use of initial capitals

Much marketing copy is spoiled by an overgenerous helping of wrongly applied initial capitals. An initial capital is a capital letter at the start of a word. You should only use one when:

> ● The word is a proper noun (London, Mary)
> ● The word is a company name (Fred's Freezers, the BBC)
> ● The word is the first in a sentence

All too often you see this:

> ✘ Farmer's Foods promise You the very Best Choice and Value for fresh vegetables, Frozen meals and Dairy produce.

Don't litter your prose with initial capitals. This use of initial capitals is wrong, ugly and distracting. The above example should, of course, read:

> ✔ Farmer's Foods promise you the very best choice and value for fresh vegetables, frozen meals and dairy produce.

*4 The 'greengrocer's apostrophe' and other apostrophes*

There is a phenomenon, jokingly referred to as the 'greengrocer's apostrophe', that is – sadly – not confined to greengrocers. Indeed it afflicts many a marketing copywriter, including those who should know better. Call in at your nearest greengrocer to see it in action:

> ✗ Pear's 70p   Apple's 60p   Grape's £1

In the last four pieces of marketing bumph I have received, there has been one or more wrongly placed apostrophe. You might see something like this:

> ✗ Chumpley's Health Farm will get you fit. We have four sauna's, two gym's and ten exercise bike's. There's even a childrens' gym. And every night we run a 60's disco.

In case you're not sure, this is how it should be:

> ✗ Chumpley's Health Farm will get you fit. We have four saunas, two gyms and ten exercise bikes. There's even a children's gym. And every night we run a '60s disco.

- *Saunas* – the plural of sauna is saunas, not sauna's. Some people think that if a word ends in 'a', the plural requires an apostrophe s. They are wrong.
- *'60s* – this is short for the 1960s. Therefore the apostrophe goes before the 60 to denote that the '19' has been dropped.
- *Gyms/bikes* – these are straight plurals so they do not need an apostrophe s.
- *Children's* – this should have an apostrophe s because it denotes the possessive: a gym for children. Normally with a possessive plural, there would be an s apostrophe (e.g. the sisters' rabbit – a rabbit belonging to some sisters), but not in the case of a word that is already pluralized. In other words, you would write

> ✔ The boys' gym [more than one boy]

> ✔ The boy's gym [one boy]

> ✔ The man's gym [one man]

> ✔ The men's gym [more than one man, but as men is already a plural, the apostrophe comes before the 's']

Use an apostrophe only:

- To denote possession – e.g. the company's policy; the shop's opening hours
- To indicate that something has been omitted, e.g. '80s (1980s); shouldn't (should not); 'til (until)

*5 Misused inverted commas*

As common as the greengrocer's apostrophe are misused inverted commas. You will often see:

> **'Free'**
> ✗ A fantastic gift 'free' with every order. But Hurry! 'Limited offer'.

Here inverted commas have been put around words to emphasize and draw attention to them. But that's not the correct use of inverted commas. They should indicate that the writer is using the word in an unusual or ironic way. For example:

> ✔ The 'free' gift actually ended up costing me a fortune!

The writer here is saying that the gift was anything but free. If you want to emphasize words, *do not* put inverted commas around them. Try using bold, underlining or italics.

*6 My husband and I*

Frequently people write (and say) 'I' when it should be 'me'. For example:

> ✗ This is a great opportunity for my husband and *I* to ...

This is wrong. But this is right:

> ✔ My husband and I think this is a great opportunity to ...

Confused? It's simple really. Take the first example. You would never write:

> ✘ This is a great opportunity for *I* ...

You would write:

> ✔ This is a great opportunity for *me* ...

If you are not sure, try saying the sentence without the 'my husband' bit. If you would say 'I', say 'my husband and I'. If you would say 'me', say 'my husband and me'.

## 7 Myself

This grammatical error becomes more common with each day that passes. You will all too often see (and hear) people write/say:

> Contact myself ...

or:

> I look forward to hearing from yourself

It should, of course, read:

> Contact me

and:

> I look forward to hearing from you

Don't make this irritating mistake yourself. Many people might not notice, but those that do won't forgive you for it!

## Grammar test

That concludes the whistlestop tour of grammar. It wasn't too painful, was it? Now for a quick test to see whether you understand the basics. Answer the following questions then check your score. If you get any wrong, make sure you understand why.

In each of the following, state whether the grammar is correct or not. If it is correct, tick it; if it is incorrect, mark it with a cross. If you think something is wrong, correct it.

1   The number of new customers we win each day are increasing rapidly.
2   All ladies' and boy's clothing is half-price.
3   Less people took up this offer than I would have hoped.
4   My colleagues and I would like to thank you for your continued custom.
5   None of us have a crystal ball. If only we had!
6   This delay will not help my colleagues or I to get our mailshot out on time.
7   We offer six types of fresh herbs with every salad dressing.
8   We offer you all this ... and more.

ANSWERS
1   ✗ It should read: '... is increasing rapidly'. 'The number' is singular, so the verb must be singular too.
2   ✗ It should read: '... and boys' clothing ...'. 'Boys' is a plural and therefore the apostrophe should come after the letter 's'.
3   ✗ It should read: '... Fewer people ...'.
4   ✔
5   ✗ It should read: '... None of us has ...'. 'None' is singular, so the verb must agree.
6   ✗ It should read: '... will not help me or my colleagues ...'.
7   ✗ It should read: '.... of fresh *herb* ...'.
8   ✔

How did you do? If you got some wrong, learn from your mistakes. If you earned a full score, well done! Your grammar is fine for the copywriting tasks ahead of you.

Now it's time to move on to English, how we use it, and how we can improve our use of it.

## English

Letters form words, words form sentences, and sentences form paragraphs. We all have access to the same twenty-six letters of the alphabet, and to the same huge vocabulary of words. Some of us can turn that raw material into compelling, powerful and memorable material: others struggle just to make themselves understood. The way you use language can set your copy apart from less skilled wordsmiths, so it is worth spending a little time analysing words and sentences.

## Words

Someone (I can't remember who) once summed up poetry as the process of selecting the right words in the right order. Doesn't that make a complex creative process sound easy? It is, of course, not easy to write good poetry, nor to produce great marketing material. Sure, half a dozen well chosen words can add up to a powerful marketing message. But which words? How do you pick the right ones? How do you know which to avoid? How do you string them together? It takes time and experience. The more you try, the better you get.

The best advice about words is never to accept the first ones that spring to mind. Examine each one. Consider whether there are better, shorter, more powerful or descriptive alternatives. The fewer words you are using, the more work they have to do. You might end up giving more thought to the four words in a hoarding headline than the 2000 words in a brochure. That's because these four words have to do the same job as 2000: they need to sell. Four ill-chosen words will stand out like a boil on the end of your nose if the sum total of your work is just four words. But four poor words hiding among 2000 is less serious.

There is no ready reckoner that will show you which word to pick: that's down to you and your skill as a copywriter. But there are some guiding principles for marketing copy:

- Use short words
- Use familiar words
- Use spoken English
- Use 'concrete words'
- Use powerful words
- Use confident words

*Short words*

Opt for shorter words over longer ones. They make your copy shorter and easier to read. Go for 'use', not 'utilize'. Choose 'live', not 'reside'. Two or three short words are better than one long one. Words of three or more syllables are harder to read, harder to recognize, and harder work.

*Familiar words*

Unfamiliar words jar and make readers struggle. If you want your writing to flow like the spoken word, avoid the unfamiliar and foreign words. Use everyday words.

*Spoken English*

Many people who speak clearly and coherently become pompous and obscure when they write. For some reason they think this is the right style to adopt. When you write, use the words you would use if you were speaking. Write 'drink', not 'beverage', 'want', not 'desire'.

*Concrete words*

A lot of marketing material is too 'flowery' and vague. Abstract words (wonderful, superb, fantastic, stylish) are overused. Try to pin your copy down with plenty of concrete words. It's the only way to convey your meaning clearly, without leaving too much to individual interpretation. Here's a passage full of abstract words:

> ✗ Our new range of Wilton carpets will knock you sideways. Available in a wide choice of colours, each carpet is stylish and luxurious. Add its hard-wearing qualities to its good looks and you'll have a carpet you simply can't beat. We're even offering some enticing credit deals into the bargain!

This is much too general. What's stylish to a carpet retailer might be completely naff to the customer. The text is so unspecific that no clear picture is produced in the reader's head. This is so much better:

> ✔ Our new range of Wilton carpets comes in 24 colours, including plains and patterns (tartans, florals and abstract designs). Each carpet has a stain-repellent coating and comes with a ten-year guarantee. Who else offers such choice *and* interest free credit?

Now we're talking! This is clear and specific. It gives the facts straight, but presents them in an appealing way.

*Powerful words*

There are various words that have been proved to be more effective than others in headlines and in other attention-grabbing situations. They include:

- New
- Free
- Advice
- Save
- Money
- Reduced
- How to
- Announcing
- Sex
- Discovery
- Now
- At last
- Proven
- You

They are not necessarily effective for any use, but they are powerful when used in headlines (for adverts; in newsletters; and in direct mail, on envelopes and in the main and subheadings of mailshots).

*Confident words*

Another way to add power and bite to your writing is to be assertive and confident. For example, don't write:

> ✗ We hope you will like your new ... and hope you will want to take up our latest offer

Write:

> ✔ We are confident you will like ... and sure you will want to take up our latest offer

Stop qualifying everything you say. Just have confidence in your products and let that confidence come through in the words you choose.

## Verbs

As you will remember from school, verbs are 'doing words' such as 'hit' and 'feel'. There are 'active' verbs and 'passive' verbs. Marketing copy benefits from being written in the 'active voice'. For example, instead of writing:

> ✗ The best furniture in town is *sold* by us

you would write:

> ✔ We *sell* the best furniture in town

You are saying the same thing in both these examples, but the second one is more succinct and has more punch. Now to sentences.

## Sentences

Let's start with structure. Well-structured sentences, comprising well-chosen words, create brilliant copy. But what makes a well-structured sentence? Well, sentences should not be looked at on their own, but together with their neighbours. If you want your writing to have rhythm, you need to look at sentence flow. While you should generally aim for fairly short sentences, you need to vary the length. Longer ones add variety. So do very short ones. (You can even use one word sentences – see below.) What is essential is that you avoid monotony.

*Inversion*

A useful device for avoiding monotony is to invert the word order. For example, instead of following the usual word order and writing:

> Many new products appear in this year's catalogue.

invert it and write:

> Appearing in this year's catalogue are many new products.

Rigidly following the usual word order, sentence after sentence, leads to dull, flat writing. Inversion can provide the necessary lift.

*One-worders*

We tend to think of sentences as comprising several words. In marketing copy you will find that one word sentences are quite acceptable. They can add pace, drama and emphasis. For example:

> What's so different about the Wellington Cabriolet Gti? Well, it's nippy. Very. And fast. Really. In fact, it's in a class of its own.

This sentence would lack pace if it were rewritten to avoid one-word sentences. It's the staccato rhythm given by the one-worders that help convey a meaning beyond the words. Here's another example of the technique in action:

> It's a cold, dark night. Wet too. You are female. Alone. And your car has just broken down. How do you feel? Scared? Unsure what to do? No need to worry. For Motor Club members help is at hand …

One word, on its own, can have more impact than the same word set among others in a longer sentence.

*Sentence types*

Essentially there are four sentence types:

- Statements – such sentences assert facts: 'You cannot buy a more powerful computer'
- Commands – these sentences tell you to do something: 'Visit our bargain basement today'
- Questions – 'Ever wondered why we're Britain's top horse club?'
- Exclamations – these are expressions of surprise: 'Hurry! Offer strictly limited'

Generally in advertising copy you will find yourself using commands. Such sentences tend to be more personal, more direct and snappier. In brochures and longer copy you will use a mixture of sentence types.

## Tenses

Generally it is better to write in the present tense, as it sounds more current and more confident. For example:

> [past tense] We have helped thousands of small businesses nation-wide to cut their stationery bills

is not as punchy and newsy as:

> [present tense] We help thousands of small businesses nationwide to cut their stationery bills

or the more active:

> Thousands of small businesses nationwide are cutting their stationery bills thanks to us

Now for a look at bias in language.

## Politically correct language

Some people like to make fun of all things 'PC' (politically correct). Laugh at your peril. If you produce sexist copy you will reduce the impact of your marketing material by offending a large part of your audience. Why take the risk? You can write great copy without offending a soul, if you follow these guidelines.

*Sexism*

Sexist language is not acceptable. Full stop. If you want to be sure to avoid it, here are some pointers:

- Females over 18 are women, not girls.
- Only use 'lady' if you would use 'gentleman' when writing about a male. Don't talk about 'lady drivers' and 'lady doctors' unless you refer also to 'gentlemen drivers' and 'gentlemen doctors'.
- Women don't just wash dishes and have babies, they go to work, mend cars, drink beer. Avoid sexual stereotypes in your writing and in the imagery you choose.

- Avoid language which discriminates against women.
- Don't use words or expressions like: 'The man in the street'; 'telephones manned by'; 'layman' etc.
- Don't write 'he/his/him' when you are writing about people in general. There are various techniques you can use to avoid sexist language:
  - One way to deal with this is to pluralize the sentence. So instead of writing: 'If a customer cannot collect the goods from our store, he can arrange to have them delivered' you could write: 'If customers cannot collect the goods from our store, they can arrange to have them delivered'.
  - Another way is to use 'they' and 'their' for the singular. (Of course, strictly speaking this is grammatically incorrect.) For example, you could write: 'If a customer cannot collect the goods from our store, they can arrange to have them delivered'.
  - Sometimes you can rewrite the sentence to avoid 'his' altogether: 'If a customer cannot collect the goods from our store, we will arrange to have them delivered' or: 'Anyone unable to collect goods from our store can have them delivered'.
  - Use 'his/hers' and 's/he' (this can be cumbersome, so use it only if none of the above work): 'If a customer cannot collect the goods from our store, s/he can arrange to have them delivered'.
- Use neutral terms whenever possible, such as chair (or chairperson), businesspeople and so on.
- Avoid feminine forms, e.g. clerkess and manageress. They sound weaker than the neutral manager and clerk.

*Racism*

- Try to avoid using 'black' in a negative way – 'black day', 'blacken the name of' etc.
- The expression 'welshing on a deal' is common, but can result in complaints from Welsh people.
- Avoid racial stereotypes – Asians don't only run corner shops, Jews and Scots are not mean.

*Ageism*

Old people do not see themselves as crotchety crinklies. Indeed a group of older people, angry at their representation on road signs (looking infirm, with walking sticks) started a campaign to have more positive images of old people, and had designs produced showing them on skateboards and doing other non-stereotypical activities. If you write about old people in a stereotyped way, you will lose customers. With an ageing population, and the growing importance of 'grey power', that's something you should take seriously.

### Able-bodiedism

Many people who have a disability dislike being referred to as 'the disabled'. They feel that this classifies them according to their disability first and foremost. They prefer the term 'people with a disability', as this sees them first as people and second as having a disability. Terms such as 'the blind' and 'the deaf' should be replaced with 'blind people' and 'deaf people'. Terms such as 'cripple' and 'handicapped' should be dropped altogether.

It is important to be 'politically correct' if you want to avoid giving offence. No business person or marketing manager would want deliberately to offend customers and send their custom elsewhere. Don't offend inadvertently through biased language.

# 6 Ten time-tested copywriting devices

In this chapter pick up powerful techniques to help you get the best from your raw material: words. Draw upon proven methods for writing lively, winning, profitable copy time after time. Find out how to use puns, write powerful headlines, and make your copy more readable.

There is no magic formula for a great piece of copy. Different copy-writers can use completely different techniques yet all come up with great words. Equally, you can use a tried and tested technique and produce lousy copy. Techniques help, there's no doubt, but they are not guarantees. You still have to work at it. Indeed, the more effort you put into your writing, the less effort your audience will need to put into reading it. And that should be your aim: copy that is so easy to read that it masks the sweat and toil that produced it. Your writing should capture the energy and ease of the spoken word (minus the ums and ahs).

If you put effort into your writing, make use of the techniques described in this chapter, and avoid the mistakes highlighted in the next one, you'll be well on your way to producing writing worth reading.

Here are ten techniques that you can use to give your copy a bit of fizz.

## 1 Alliteration

Alliteration is the use of similar sounds at the beginning of neigh-bouring words, for example:

> *M*urphy's *M*uffins are *m*unchy and *m*ore-ish!

The best alliteration involves more than just the repeating of sounds. It is far more subtle, yet it achieves the same effect: words that trip off the tongue.

Some sounds are better for alliteration than others, according to linguisticians. Those made by temporarily stopping the air stream with your tongue or lips are best – p, b, m, n, t, d, k, and g.

## 2 Puns

The pun is one of the most common devices in marketing copy, especially for headlines in adverts and articles. Puns can be really effective, witty and memorable. They can be a great outlet for a creative copywriter fascinated by words and their meaning. Here are some real examples of puns in action:

> HURRY OVERTURE NEAREST PHONE
> [telephone booking service for an orchestra's winter season]

> DRAMATIC SAVINGS BARD NONE
> [half-price ticket offer by the Royal Shakespeare Company]

> STICK A TENOR IN SOMEONE'S CARD THIS CHRISTMAS
> [advert for theatre gift vouchers]

> A BANK FOR PEOPLE WITH VERY LITTLE INTEREST IN BANKS
> [advert for a high-interest bank account]

Jokes and riddles can be a great source of puns. Take these two:

Q: What's the difference between a jeweller and a jailer?
A: A jeweller *sells* watches but a jailer watches *cells*.

Q: What is the difference between a nurse and a seamstress?
A: A nurse dresses *cuts* but a seamstress *cuts* dresses.

Look at puns and analyse how they work. If you are at a loss for ideas, see if puns can work for you. But a word of warning. Beware the unintentional puns. For example:

> NEW! Crash course in driving

> We dispense with accuracy [advert for pharmacy]

> Let your children watch as we bake their nan in front of them
> [from the family menu at an Indian restaurant]

Any puns you use should be intentional, not accidental!

## 3 Assonance

Assonance is the repetition of vowel sounds to form an incomplete rhyme. It is far more subtle than alliteration and only works with vowels in stressed syllables. A famous example is the slogan for the American president Eisenhower (nicknamed 'Ike'):

I like Ike

A political commentator of the time adapted this to make the point that some people were not sure what policies Eisenhower actually believed in. He came up with this:

I like Ike, but what does Ike like?

Another example from the USA – the former President Richard ('Dicky') Nixon was known by some as 'Tricky Dicky'.

## 4 Rhyme

You can also use old-fashioned rhyme. For example:

Know of a benefit rip-off? Give us a telephone tip-off. Call the Beat-A-Cheat Line
[an advert for the government's clampdown on benefits fraud]

Deals on Wheels
[headline for customer newsletter article on special offers on cars]

Rhyme is about *sound*, not spelling. As a result, some adverts using rhyme are better as broadcast ads than on the page.

## 5 Ellipsis

Ellipsis is a technique often used in marketing copy, perhaps because it is a way of involving your reader in your writing (if used successfully). To produce an ellipsis you need to omit a word or words which the reader must supply. Clearly the missing words must be obvious, otherwise your copy would be meaningless. For example:

> Hidden inside there's … No, that would be telling
> [an advert for Rolo truffles]

You are (I guess) meant to deduce that hidden inside the Rolo truffle there's a yummy and tasty filling so good it's best kept a secret. Ellipses allow you to say a lot (or to suggest a lot) without using a lot of words. It's more a case of what you don't say. Ellipsis is also the name for the punctuation mark '…' (dot dot dot) used in the example above. You don't need to use ellipses in order to produce an elliptical sentence. Take this example:

> ✔ They don't carry her as far as they used to. But we do.

As straight text this advert makes no sense. But combined with a close-up photo of an elderly woman's legs, supported by a walking stick, and the London Underground's logo, we understand the message immediately. It is a short and powerful way of conveying a message and engaging readers by getting them to interpret it. This is a really effective use of ellipsis, as you can see if you compare it with the same message written without this technique.

> ✗ An elderly woman's legs don't carry her as far as they used to. But we at the London Underground do.

This lacks the punch and cleverness of the first example.

Here's another example along similar lines. This is for a restaurant at a smart hotel. The photograph shows a crisp white tablecloth set for dinner and the headline reads:

> This is starched. Our service isn't

Another way of using ellipsis is to leave out letters, not whole words, for example:

> [advert for gardeners]
> If you think your manure is a pile of old S**T, try ours

This method can be used to enable you to say rude things without causing too much offence.

## 6 Homonyms

A homonym is a word that is spelt the same as another, yet has a different meaning. You can use homonyms to write witty copy. A radio advert with a voice-over by Vincent Price (who usually played a vampire in the many horror films he starred in) said:

> You'll love the London Dungeon. I'll *stake* my heart on it

This is a good example of a homonym being used as a clever pun: 'stake' meaning both a wager and a sharp wooden stick used for killing vampires. As it happens, this is also a homophone (a word that sounds the same as another, but with a different meaning and some-times – though not in this case – a different spelling). You can read more about homophones in Chapter 11. Homonyms and homo-phones work well in headlines.

## 7 Antonyms

An antonym is a word that means the opposite (as opposed to a synonym, which is a word that has the same meaning). Antonyms work well in copy, particularly in adverts and slogans, though they can be used to effect in most copywriting assignments. For example:

> A *little* car with a *big* personality

> *Overspill* your trolley, *underspend* your budget
> [ad for a supermarket]

> *High* in taste, *low* in fat

> A *big* newspaper for a *small* coin
> [used when *The Sun* reduced its price to 20p]

> Before you *check in, check out* our prices
> [ad for duty-free airport shopping]

You can use this technique with words that are not, strictly speaking, antonyms. For example:

> Takes *minutes*, lasts *weeks*
> [a hair-removing cream]

> *Half* the size, *twice* the benefit
> [slogan for a new, smaller air freshener]

## 8 Unexpected deviance

This term sounds like an arrestable offence! It's actually a very useful copywriting device. You have a list or a series of sentences, each following a pattern. The last one in the list deviates unexpectedly from that pattern, for example:

> **100%** customer service
> **100%** quality
> **100%** choice
> **0%** finance

or:

> Top brands
> Top service
> Top style
> Bottom prices

or, more subtle:

> Top brands
> Top service
> Top style
> Top that!

or this real-life example, from Virgin Direct Personal Financial Service:

> Good quality, good value, good service and good riddance to salesmen!

## 9 Malapropisms

A malapropism is where a common expression is altered unintentionally, giving it a comic or ludicrous interpretation. (It comes from Mrs Malaprop, a character from Sheridan's play, *The Rivals*.) By changing a word or sound, the original meaning is quite altered. Hilda Ogden in television's *Coronation Street* was famous for her malapropisms, such as calling her mural a 'murial'. Recently a woman noted for putting on airs and graces told me that as her son had been awarded an honours degree, she would be going to his *granulation* ceremony! Other examples I have heard lately include:

- I am on tender hooks
- That was a non-secateur
- She is a sincophant
- That wench is used lifting heavy loads

Why not use malapropisms intentionally to produce witty and talked-about adverts? It is a technique that takes some skill, but can work really well.

## 10 Spoonerisms

In the same vein as malapropisms are spoonerisms, named after the Reverend William Spooner. This academic and cleric was forever getting his words mixed up. Once, instead of announcing a toast to 'our dear old queen' he proposed: 'Let us drink to the queer old dean'! Spoonerisms can be used to great effect, if you can find an opportunity. Certainly you should experiment with spoonerisms and malapropisms if you are at a loss for a creative solution. See what you can come up with. My favourite is: a scoop of Boy Trouts (a troop of Boy Scouts).

# 7 Common copywriting mistakes and how to avoid them

Every day dreadful copy makes it into print, damaging organizations' reputations and annoying customers. Don't fall foul of the common copywriting errors. This chapter will alert you to the most frequent mistakes made by wannabe copywriters – from clichés and tautology to hype and verbosity – and will advise on how to avoid them.

Good copy comes as much from knowing what to avoid as from understanding what should be done. For every copywriting *must* there are probably two *must nots*. Do the *dos*, avoid the *don'ts* and you'll be a lot closer to really effective copy.

Good copy is lively, punchy, to the point. It grabs attention and grips the reader. Ineffective copy does the opposite. But what makes a piece of writing ineffective? What should you avoid?

## 1 Over-long text

Lengthy copy is OK, depending on what you are writing and who for. But text that is too long is definitely not.

> - It's unnecessarily time-consuming, taking up too much of your reader's time
> - If it's too long, it's probably boring too
> - It will take up more space and might therefore cost more to print
> - It's a sign of sloppy thinking and poor planning
> - It is unlikely that a reader will stick with it to the end

Your writing should be as long as it needs to be and no longer. Prune wordy copy. Cut out repetition. Delete superfluous words. End up with a trimmer, leaner version that packs more punch.

## 2 Marketing clichés

A cliché is an 'off-the-shelf' overused expression or phrase. A lot of the marketing material I see is littered with clichés. Some publicity is little more than a string of clichés linked by the occasional conjunction. If you want your writing to stand out, to be fresh and vital, avoid all clichés. They will add nothing. Here are some of the most common marketing clichés. Never use them.

- The best that money can buy
- An opportunity not to be missed
- Never to be repeated
- Chance/offer of a lifetime
- A new concept in home entertainment
- A warm welcome awaits you at ...
- A dream holiday/kitchen
- A unique opportunity
- We are delighted to announce
- It is our pleasure to offer you
- A truly amazing
- As a valued customer

## 3 General clichés

A master of straight-talking, the late Sir Ernest Gowers wrote in his best-selling *The Complete Plain Words*: 'A cliché then is by definition a bad thing, not to be employed by self-respecting writers.' How true! Yet we seem to live by clichés when we speak and when we write. Ban yourself from using them and see how you struggle! The cliché is a lazy solution and should be avoided by copywriters. Be imaginative. Don't dredge up common and overused phrases: invent your own. Make your copy fresh and readable, not stale and hackneyed.

Here's an example of the type of thing you should avoid, albeit a rather exaggerated one:

> ✗ We might all be enjoying this Indian summer, with winter thoughts far from our mind. But the colder months are just round the corner. Keep warm as toast this winter with a 'living flame' gas fire. During the next cold snap your neighbours will be green with envy when they see how cosy your lounge is compared with their own. So if you want to be snug as a bug in a rug when Jack Frost calls, get your living flame brochure now.

Of course, you can turn clichés on their head, transforming them into witty ditties. Take this example:

> ✔ The Bucks Start Here
> [advert for an investment product]

## 4 Verbosity

Verbosity is the copywriter's enemy. Verbose words and phrases can creep up on the inexperienced writer, leaving their copy flat and flabby. If you want fitter, leaner text, check your work for verbosity. Here are some of the most common examples of verbosity you will come across. Avoid them:

| *Flabby* | *Fit* |
|---|---|
| at this point in time | now |
| with regard to/regarding/pertaining to | about |
| in connection with | about |
| on a regular basis | regularly |
| please find enclosed | I enclose |
| subsequent to | after |
| inform | tell |
| terminate | end |
| commence | start/begin |
| reside | live |
| endeavour | try |
| assist | help |
| until such time as | until |
| desire | want |
| in terms of | rewrite to avoid, if possible |
| relocate | move |
| refreshment facilities | bar/café/restaurant |
| parking facilities | parking |
| employment on a part time basis | part-time work |
| prior to | before |
| proceed | go/walk etc. |
| purchase | buy |
| utilize | use |
| for the purpose of | for |
| in order to | to |
| we would be grateful if | please |
| executive summary | summary |
| owing to the fact that | because |
| in the event that | if |
| in spite of the fact that | although |
| in the majority of cases | usually |

The above list is not exhaustive, but you get the idea. I could go on and on and on … Always use short, familiar words rather than longer phrases or 'official' terms – even in official writing. Keep your copy sharp and crisp.

## 5 Redundancy/tautology

Redundancy (sometimes known as tautology) is where you use superfluous words, needlessly repeating an idea. The following are examples of redundancy and should be avoided. (The redundant word(s) can be found in parentheses.)

- Join (together)
- Meet (up with)
- Divide (up)
- Separate (out)
- Complete the coupon and return (back) to us
- (Free) gifts
- Fantastic (new) innovation
- Don't miss (out on) this fantastic offer
- Why not try it (out) using our free offer
- (Advance) planning
- (Unfilled) vacancy
- Available in a range of (different) colours – or available in (a range of) different colours

Redundancy is a sign of sloppy writing and a waste of space. Check that your writing is free of it.

## 6 Very

Using the word 'very' can be a weak way of expressing yourself. And the more you use it, the weaker it becomes. So try to avoid it. Usually there are better ways of expressing intensity than tacking 'very' before an adjective. For example, 'very hot' is better described as: baking; sweltering; scorching; sizzling … 'Very tired' is weaker than: exhausted; fatigued; worn out; done in; weary; blitzed; zonked.

## 7 Ambiguity

For copy to be successful, what you write must be what they read. Put another way, the message you send is the same as the message received. Never assume that the two coincide: they frequently do not.

It is not unusual even for professionally written copy to contain ambiguity – where your words have two or more meanings or interpretations, or the meaning is unclear. For example:

> For an annual subscription of just £20 you can get *Gardening Times* delivered direct to your door, bi-monthly.

Does this mean that you get a magazine every two months, or twice every month? It makes a big difference! Here's another example:

> Introducing two great new products:
> ● our precision tile cutter and
> ● our one-step grout
> Both cost just £20 …

£20 each? £20 for the two? If your wording is ambiguous you will lose sales. People will not have the time or inclination to write or phone to check the details, so they won't order. Or they might equate sloppy writing with a sloppy product. Either way, you lose.

If you are a very skilful writer you can deliberately use ambiguity to create clever and memorable copy, as in this example from a TV advert:

> A woman offers a rather conceited man some coffee during a business meeting. He asks if she has decaffeinated coffee. She makes the coffee and gives it to the man, who tastes it.
> *Man:* I see you didn't have decaffeinated then!
> *Woman:* No, but you did.

At first the viewer takes the wrong meaning from the man's comment. They assume that he has been given non-decaffeinated coffee. When the woman speaks we realize that the coffee he had was in fact decaffeinated. This is a very clever way of saying: 'Our decaffeinated coffee is so good it has all the taste of non-decaffeinated coffee.' Ambiguity in this context is a powerful tool; in any other it is a grave mistake.

## 8 Hype

Too much marketing material is little more than hype. It is full of exaggerated, misleading, or even false claims. I understand how tempting it can be for copywriters to exaggerate the benefits of their product, particularly if it is actually rather dull. Hyping enables a copywriter to turn a dreary assignment into one with a bit more zip. But overselling must be avoided. It only leads to disappointment when your readers inevitably discover that your claims were nothing more than puffery. Disappointment creates unhappy customers, and unhappy customers eventually lead to a business's downfall.

On a Turkish holiday I saw an exotic-sounding item on a restaurant menu. I asked the waiter what it was and he explained that it was a delicious dessert made with the finest fresh produce: eggs, cane sugar, milk, flour and one or two other ingredients. It sounded wonderful and I ordered one. But what did I get? A dried-up square of sponge cake! The goods failed to live up to the description. I could forgive the waiter; he was, after all, communicating in a foreign language. But what's your excuse?

Here are two examples of hype:

> A traditional unleavened bread lightly stroked with olive oil, smothered with a delicious paste made from fresh Italian tomatoes, topped with succulent buffalo cheese and sprinkled with sundried rosemary and basil, then baked in special ovens
> [a frozen pizza packaging]

> [flyer for a craft and DIY magazine]
> [picture of ordinary flower display] Make a bewitching topiary

> [photo of two wooden shelves] Conjure up a set of attractive and stylish shelves that will amaze and impress

## 9 Pomposity

Perfectly nice people so often take on a pompous air when they pick up a pen and try to write. These otherwise down-to-earth people come across as pompous asses, with their high-falutin language or obsequious phrases. This stems from a belief, drummed into many of us at school, that the written word should be formal and grand-sounding. I'm not convinced that there is a place for this kind of writing in any situation, but certainly there is no room for it in copywriting. It sounds ridiculous, as you can see in the following example, which, though fictitious, is all too typical of what is produced:

> **CHUMBERS RESTAURANT**
> The discerning client will appreciate the effort the Chumbers
> team put into making the dining experience at our restaurant
> unforgettable. Maitre d' prides himself on the crisp, starched
> tablecloths on which our guests are served, silver service of course,
> a delectable luncheon. Connoisseurs will delight at our extensive
> winelist. Those with a sweet tooth will be truly overjoyed at the
> choice of desserts we can offer.

## 10 Waffle

Call it what you like, waffle or padding dilutes the impact of your
message. The more you pad your words, the less the important
sections stand out. Your message gets lost in a mass of cotton wool.
As a result you are more likely to lose your reader.

Here's an example of waffle. The waffley words are in square
brackets.

> ✗ [We would like to point out that] no other company offers
> [you] the quality and range of products that we do. [You should
> note that] this offer is only available for a limited [period of] time.

This example demonstrates very clearly how a simple message of just
twenty-two words can get lost in waffle that adds nothing and brings
the word count to a less manageable thirty-six.

## 11 Repetition

Repetition of the same words and phrases is a sign of sloppy writing.
It grates on the reader and distracts them from your message. Here's
a typical example (with repeated words and phrases in italics):

> We are delighted to announce the *opening* of another Johnston's
> Toy Superstore. This year we have *opened* 20 stores across *Britain,*
> bringing the total number of *stores* to 100 in *Britain.* That means
> there will be a *store near* you. To *find out* where your *nearest*
> Superstore is, and to *find out* its *opening* hours, take a look at the
> back page of this catalogue where you will *find* all the information
> you need.

Repetition of this sort is boring and should be avoided. There are
times when repetition can work to your advantage in marketing copy,
reinforcing your message. Here's an example:

> As a very special customer we'd like to make you a very special offer. We're Britain's best computer dealer, so you'd expect us to offer the best equipment at the best prices.

> 24 hours to play, 24 months to pay [car advert offering a day's test drive and two years' interest-free credit]

> NO salesmen. NO commission. NO jargon. NO hassle.
> [advert for a personal equity plan]

When used deliberately, repetition can emphasize the point and drive home the message. But if used by default it may have the opposite effect.

The eleven common copywriting mistakes above are easily avoided if you take sufficient care. But remember that they are not the only things you need to steer clear of. Here are some others you should avoid.

## Nine commonly misused words

Many people misuse words in everyday speech. There is no excuse for copywriters to do this. After all, the writer has the benefit of time for careful consideration and selection of words. Here are nine words that are commonly misused, both in spoken and written English. Never be guilty of misusing them yourself:

1 *Anticipating:* Many people use this word when they actually mean expecting. For example, they will write: 'We anticipate that you will receive your goods in the next week.' Anticipating requires some action to bring about a particular outcome. If you believe that you will get a record number of orders, you could take on more staff to cope with the extra demand. You could then quite rightly claim to have anticipated the demand.

2 *Presently:* This does not mean that you are doing something at the moment (i.e. currently), it means that you will do it soon, e.g. We will presently be introducing our new season's range.

3 *Verbal:* Too often this is used instead of 'oral'. Verbal involves words, which can be spoken or written. Oral refers purely to the spoken word.

4 *Less/fewer:* fewer means 'not so many' while less means 'not so

much'. Therefore you would say: 'Our goods cost you less' and 'Our competitors have fewer outlets'.

5 *Aggravate:* This means to make worse. If you scratch a spot you will aggravate it. It does not mean the same as irritate or annoy!

6 *Imply/infer:* People infer things from what others have said (or written). If someone hints at something, but does not say it directly, they are implying.

7 *Its/it's:* Although I am not a pedant when it comes to grammar, this really is my pet hate and confusion of the two is inexcusable. 'It's' is short for 'it is' – for example: It's a great place to shop; it's a bargain-hunter's paradise. In each case the 'it's' can be substituted with an 'it is'. 'Its' means something quite different. It is the possessive form of 'it' – for example: You'll love its ambience; where's its lid gone?

8 *Literally:* I frequently hear people say things such as 'I'm literally over a barrel' or 'It's literally on my doorstep'. The only things likely to be literally on your doorstep are visitors ringing your doorbell or bottles of milk! If you are literally over a barrel, then you must have a barrel beneath you, which is unlikely. And if you literally die laughing, you'll be literally six feet under.

9 *Disinterested/not interested:* If you are disinterested, you are impartial. Disinterested, therefore, does not mean not interested. On the contrary, one is interested, but has no axe to grind.

## No offence intended

Copy that offends will not sell. It is easy for a copywriter to cause offence unintentionally, so always err on the side of caution. A crane hire company wanted to produce an advert for the trade press aimed at getting contractors to hire from a reputable firm if they wanted to avoid getting landed with potentially dangerous equipment. Their advert showed a smiling girl next to an open car door, with the headline: 'Don't take lifts from strangers!'. Following a complaint, the ASA (Advertising Standards Authority) considered the advert and deemed it unsuitable, given the social concern about child abduction. What in particular should you avoid for fear of causing offence?

*1 Four letter words*

Bad language in your copy is to be avoided, even if it is meant humorously. Attitude research carried out by the Advertising Standards Authority showed that even relatively mild swear words like pillock, git, bloody and damn were found to be unacceptable in posters and other advertising. Even those who themselves swear may find expletives offensive in other people's writing. An advert for Virgin cola had a complaint against it upheld, even though the offending word was not in English. The ad, appearing on the day of the Euro '96 England versus Spain football match, in a tabloid's sports pages, read: 'Eres una mierda aaaaargh! Trans: What a fine Spanish team you are!'. Of course, its real meaning is a little coarser (consult your Spanish dictionary!). So tread carefully and be sensitive.

### 2 No sex please, we're British

You've probably heard the expression 'sex sells'. When writing copy you should be reminded that sex also offends. Independent research carried out in 1996 on behalf of the Advertising Standards Authority found that 64 per cent of respondents were offended by adverts that portrayed women as sex objects. This popular style of advertising in the 1960s and 1970s was on the wane, but now appears to be making a comeback, despite this being the decade of political correctness. The same research found that people are also offended by sexually explicit advertising, which makes many people feel embarrassed or uncomfortable.

Sex should not be used as an attention-grabber, as in this real-life example:

> ✗ [photograph of young woman leaning against piano wearing a short dress, which had ridden up to expose part of her bare buttocks. Captioned:]
>
> GENTLEMEN NOW WE HAVE YOUR ATTENTION, WE WOULD LIKE TO ANNOUNCE THE ARRIVAL OF THE NEW SEASON COLLECTIONS ...

Sex used in this way amounts to poor copy on two counts. First, it causes offence and thus loses you custom. Second, the picture might well attract attention, but does the advert arouse interest in the product, desire to own the product, and action to buy the product? No. Sex might attract attention, but on its own it cannot achieve a sale for you.

There are always a few people who see sexual innuendo where none exists. You need not worry too much about these people. When Durex ran an advert for condoms on the London Underground it provoked some bizarre complaints. The ad showed an embracing couple and a 'thought bubble'. One person complained that the thought bubble seemed to represent discharged semen! Another said that the person sitting below the ad would be seen to be thinking about sex! You can't please them all!

### 3 A kiss of death

Death is a no-go area (unless you are promoting an undertaker's service, and even then great sensitivity is required). An advert for a song called 'Roll Over and Die' showed a large kitchen knife beside the song lyrics, which included 'If you can't take this there's only one way out ...' and continued in this vein. Complaints to the Advertising Standards Authority resulted.

In another case (which again prompted complaints to the Authority), an advert offered West End offices rent-free, adding: 'Imagine the consequences if you miss this opportunity.' This was accompanied by a photo of a man holding a pistol to his head.

### 4 Telling fibs

If you produce copy that is misleading or downright dishonest, you will land yourself and your company in trouble. A hotel claimed to be 'Torquay's highest rated seafront 3 star hotel', despite there being another equally rated seafront hotel nearby. If you write misleading copy you will lose custom – guaranteed.

### 5 Suspect humour

Humour is a subjective matter. Personally I have a rather juvenile sense of humour, but I am aware that this is not shared by everyone. When writing for others, you need to be mindful of sensitivities. What's funny to you may be distressing to others. For example, I was amused by an advert for a soft drink that showed a woman leaning over a man and kissing him. The headline read: 'If I suck hard enough I might get my Irn-Bru back.' It made me laugh, but it made forty-six people angry enough to complain to the Advertising Standards Authority.

Humour can be a fantastic creative device, and some of our most successful ads have been based on it. But you have to be very talented to use humour, and even the professionals sometimes get it wrong. An advert written for IBM by the big ad agency, Ogilvy and Mather, fell into this category. It claimed that a computer's speakers were a 'thundering 30-watt', 'wall-shaking' and that they were 'one way to meet the neighbours'. This approach was not shared by the person who reported them to the Advertising Standards Authority, nor by the Authority itself, who considered that the ad condoned noise pollution.

### 6 Controversy

Some companies thrive on controversy. The name Benetton springs to mind. But you have to be a very clever copywriter, and a company willing to build its image around controversy, to take this sort of risk. As a general rule it is best to avoid it. (That doesn't mean you have to be bland!) An advert for an Internet access provider pictured a pill above the headline: 'We supply speed to techno-junkies'. The reference to illegal drugs was considered inappropriate and the advertisers were asked to amend their advert.

### 7 Religion

It is said that if people wish to remain friends, they should avoid discussing religion and politics. Certainly religious allusion in copy can land you in trouble. People take religion very seriously and don't like it being used in anything as trivial and consumerist as marketing material. Readers of the Advertising Standards Authority's *Monthly Report* will be aware that copy that in any way uses religious allusion is strongly objected to by some members of the public. Don't risk offending. Steer clear of religion (unless you are promoting a church!)

# 8 Criticism and analysis

To be a really good copywriter you need to be interested in the subject of copywriting. You must understand what works, what fails, what stands out as really great copy and why. In short, you need finely tuned critical skills, both to assess your own work and to learn from others. This chapter will help you develop these skills.

Do you often look at a piece of marketing material and think: 'That's brilliant. I wish I'd written that!'? You do? Good. But if you don't – it's time you started. Professional copywriters are 'copy-aware'. They are interested in copy, especially other people's. That's how you need to be. You should be constantly on the lookout for other people's copy, ever eager to dissect it, to analyse it, to understand it, to be critical of it, to learn from it. Never let marketing copy wash over you. Don't idly eye adverts or scan direct mailshots. Stop looking at copy as a punter and start applying your professional analytical skills to it. Regard yourself as a copy scientist. Identify the techniques used. Understand what makes a particular piece of writing great. Or what makes another one mediocre.

Once you become copy-aware you will find that your ability to write good copy increases. Copywriting will become more instinctive. This will subconsciously influence and improve your own work. You will find yourself in an upward spiral, writing ever better copy and gaining in confidence as your ability grows. Doesn't that sound good! It's true too. Once you reach the state of 'copy-aware' you will see a vast improvement to your own work for remarkably little effort.

Becoming copy-aware is easy. Get hold of a pile of newspapers and magazines and cut out the ads in them. Place effective ads in one pile and poor ads in another. Do the same with brochures, direct mail and other marketing material. Nip out with a camera and photograph billboards, adverts on buses and in shop windows. Look through the good materials and try to understand why they are good. Has the copywriter used particular techniques that are well suited to the medium? Have they approached the task from a novel or innovative angle? Do words and pictures work in harmony? Really take the material apart. Try to understand where the copywriter is coming from. Now repeat the process with the poor publicity material. What makes something inferior? Is it too long? Wrong language? Wrong message? Be specific. What makes it poorer? Have a go at rewriting the bad examples if you have time. What techniques can you use to spice up flat copy or to make weak material hard-hitting?

Gathering together a wide range of copy takes time. To get you started why not have a go with the following examples? I have put together a mix of real and made-up examples of good and bad copy. The made-up examples are based on real copy, so they do show the sort of marketing material being turned out by businesses.

Read through the following examples. For the examples of bad copy, write down:

---

- What is wrong with each one (be as detailed as possible)
- Whether there is anything good/any redeeming features (specify what)

---

(When you have worked through the examples, take a look at the end of the chapter to compare your notes with mine.)

## The bad

*Example 1*

This is made up from real extracts of a publicity brochure for a rather down-at-heel hotel in Earl's Court, London. (I have changed the name of the hotel.)

---

Dear guest,

On behalf of the Management and Staff, may I take this opportunity to welcome you to the Boswall Park Hotel ...

We want to make your visit to the Boswall Park Hotel a memorable occasion, and it is our desire that every guest should receive entire satisfaction during their stay. Our caring and friendly staff will attend to your every comfort, always with the personalized style that will endear you to our hotel.

This Guest Directory of Hotel Services in your bedroom, describes all other facilities available in the Hotel. This elegant international hotel offers the discerning traveller the attention to detail and standards of service they would expect. Bedrooms have been beautifully designed and furnished to the highest standard of luxury. All bedrooms feature the modern-day facilities expected of a luxury hotel, including a hair dryer and trouser press. The Tulip Bar has a superb collection of beverages and is the perfect venue for a relaxation ...

---

Our aim is to provide the highest standards of service and hospitality, with the comfort and facilities you would expect of modern luxury hotels, while preserving the traditional character of the properties themselves. If you wish to have any further information please do not hesitate to contact myself or any member of my staff. I take this opportunity to wish you a very enjoyable stay at the Boswall Park Hotel.

*Example 2*

This is a (fictitious) newspaper advert for a new magazine.

*OPTIONS:* GET IT!

*Options* is the newest magazine to hit newsagents. Majoring on information every home-owner will want, from new wallpaper to getting a better deal on your mortgage, *Options* will have all the answers ... and more! Free gift with first issue. Buy it today!

*Example 3*

This is a fictitious direct mail letter:

Dear Mrs Smith,

Here is an opportunity not to be missed. We are offering you the chance of a lifetime – a dream cruise on the Nile. Yes, this fantastic trip is the first prize in an exclusive competition being offered to anyone ordering from the enclosed catalogue before the end of December.

Imagine it. Relaxing on a sun lounger on the deck of a five-star luxury cruise boat as you glide past historic temples. Visit the treasures of Tutankhamun, the temple of Philae, the Colossi of Memnon. Haggle in the souks and bazaars. Marvel at the splendours of the ancient world. All this can be yours if your entry is lucky enough to be picked. Anyone ordering from the catalogue will automatically be entered in the draw.

You will see from the catalogue that we offer an unrivalled range of travel goods. Everything from mosquito repellent to travel plugs. From suitcases to passport holders. Every item you could possibly need for holidays at home and abroad can be found in our catalogue. So place your order now!

Yours sincerely

Thomas Tobias
Promotions Manager

## The good

Sometimes it can be a confidence boost to see just how badly other people write! You realize that your skills are better than you thought. But now for a look at some good copy, again featuring a mix of real and made-up examples. Work out what it is that makes the copy effective. Compare notes with me at the end of the chapter.

*Example 1*

[The headline from an advert for a development of luxury flats, which showed someone in front of the flats playing a saxophone]

Makes Other Penthouses Sound A Little Flat!

*Example 2*

[slogan from advert for an upright vacuum cleaner]

The Upright that's Downright Good

*Example 3*

[extract from an article in a customer newsletter. Produced by a fictitious company running theme parks and leisure complexes]

KEEP YOUR KIDS ENTERTAINED
**Six quick, easy and cheap ways to avoid boredom this summer**

School holidays can be great fun ... until the boredom sets in. Day after day of the kids under your feet, getting into mischief, running out of things to keep them occupied. Despair not! Make this summer different. Give your children a time to remember, without breaking the bank.

Here are half a dozen ways of keeping your under-12s entertained.

1  CRAFTWORK
Kids love craftwork. Save up all your old card, ribbon, washing up liquid bottles, cereal boxes, loo roll tubes etc. Buy a huge tub of glue, a ball of string and a selection of poster paints. Although they might end up making an almighty mess, your children will be kept busy for hours – and you'll be nurturing their creative side.
Cost: £7.50 for enough materials to keep four children busy for days

> ## 2 TOMMY'S THEME PARK
> Escape the real world and enter the realms of fantasy at Tommy's Theme Park. Experience weightlessness on our moon walk. Swim with crocodiles in our swamp simulator. Chat with a dinosaur in our primeval forest. Adults and children will love every minute of it.
> Cost: £25 for two adults and two children
>
> ## 3 NATURE TRAIL
> Draw up a list of items and send your children off on a nature trail to find them. You might want to include: toadstools; buttercups; daisies; ivy; moss; ants; spiders; beetles. Have a prize for the child who finds all the items first. Have runner-up prizes for everyone else to prevent punch-ups afterwards!
> Cost: none

## Comparing notes

If you have worked through the examples in this chapter, compare your findings with mine.

## The bad

*Example 1: Hotel brochure*

This example is really dreadful, yet it is all too typical of marketing material written in-house. It breaks all the rules of good copy and has no redeeming features.

> - *Too wordy* – for example, why write: 'On behalf of the Management and Staff, may I take this opportunity to welcome you to the Boswall Park Hotel ...' when it's more effective simply to write: 'Welcome to the Boswall Park Hotel.'
> - *Too stuffy* – 'on behalf of', 'may I take this opportunity', etc.
> - *Too pompous* – 'it is our desire' etc.
> - *Stating the obvious* – 'This Guest Directory of Hotel Services in your bedroom ...' You are in your bedroom reading a leaflet called Directory of Hotel Services. You don't need to be told that! Nor do you need to be told that the bar sells 'beverages'.
> - *Inappropriate initial capitalization* – words like Staff, Hotel Services, etc. do not need capital letters unless they are at the beginning of a sentence.
> - *Obsequiousness* – 'the discerning traveller'.
> - *Ridiculous claims* – hairdryers and trouser presses are hardly the height of luxury!

- *Flabbiness* – see in particular the sentence: 'Our aim is to provide the highest standards of service and hospitality, with the comfort and facilities you would expect of modern luxury hotels, while preserving the traditional character of the properties themselves.'
- *Hype* – claiming that a shabby hotel in Earl's Court is a luxury, elegant international hotel is tommyrot and diminishes any truth in what you write.

*Example 2: advert for new magazine*

On the plus side, this advert is not too wordy. But that's probably its only redeeming feature!

- *Headline* – the headline fails to do its job. It does not attract the attention of people who are interested in their homes
- *Incomplete* – the advert mentions a free gift but fails to say what it is. It does not mention frequency of publication
- *Tense* – the use of the present tense would give the copy a lift
- *Call to action* – the 'Buy it today!' call to action is not sufficient. You need to say where it can be bought and for how much

Here's the ad again, and underneath it is a better alternative:

*OPTIONS:* GET IT!

*Options* is the newest magazine to hit newsagents. Majoring on information every home-owner will want, from new wallpaper to getting a better deal on your mortgage, *Options* will have all the answers ... and more! Free gift with first issue. Buy it today!

**HOME-OWNERS: NEW MAGAZINE AND FREE GIFT**

Want to save money on your mortgage? Like to know about best buys in home furnishings? Then *Options* is for you! Packed full of tips and advice on every aspect of owning a home, from the financial side through to interior design, it is available monthly at all branches of WH Smith and John Menzies. Issue 1 is on sale now – with free 'star' stencil. Don't miss it!

In the second version the target audience for the magazine is flagged up in the headline, along with the incentive (the free gift). It therefore attracts that all-important attention straight off. It goes on to fill in details in an enticing way.

*Example 3: direct mail letter promoting travel catalogue*

What is being sold? An Egyptian cruise or holiday goods? You could be forgiven for thinking that the holiday was what was being sold, not the goods in the mail order catalogue. If I were to have to rewrite the letter, I would produce something more along the following lines:

---

Dear Mrs Smith,

### LIKE TRAVELLING? THEN YOU'LL LOVE
### THIS CATALOGUE
**It might even win you a trip to Egypt!**

If you like to travel – at home or abroad – you'll love what's in our new catalogue. Every item a traveller could possibly want can be found in the pages of the enclosed catalogue. From tummy pills to travel plugs, and mosquito nets to medical insurance, it's all here. What's more, if you place an order before the end of December, we'll automatically enter you in our prize draw to win a family Nile cruise.

Imagine it. Relaxing on a sun lounger on the deck of a five-star luxury cruise boat as you glide past historic temples. Visit the treasures of Tutankhamun, the temple of Philae, the Colossi of Memnon. Haggle in the souks and bazaars. Marvel at the splendours of the ancient world. Place an order and your family could enjoy all this.

Take a look through the catalogue. We're sure you will be delighted with our unrivalled range and affordable prices. And remember, you might get more than you bargained for if your named is picked out of the hat!

Yours sincerely


Thomas Tobias
Promotions Manager

PS Remember to place your order by the end of December if you want to enter our exclusive draw for a family trip to Egypt

---

The original version focused too much on the prize draw, mentioning the product (the catalogue) almost incidentally. It failed to use direct mail techniques, such as the headline and post-script to flag up and reinforce the message. Additionally, the first part of the letter was filled with marketing clichés. In its favour, the middle paragraph was not too bad. The problem is that no one will read as far as a middle paragraph unless you get the preceding paragraphs right.

## The good

*Example 1: advert for penthouse flats*

This headline is a great illustration of good copy. A few simple words combine to form an attention-grabbing headline that succinctly conveys some key messages.

- *Clever* – a neat little pun on the words 'little flat'
- *Succinct* – a few words get the point across
- *Key messages* – a short headline conveys two key messages, namely: (a) penthouses for sale (the word penthouse conjuring up images of luxury) and (b) other properties are inferior. It does this in an oblique, but nevertheless hard-hitting, way

*Example 2: vacuum cleaner slogan*

This is everything a slogan should be.

- *Clever* – slogans need to be memorable and this one is, thanks to its clever play on words: upright/downright
- *Key messages* – it gets across the message that it is an upright cleaner and that it is a very good cleaner
- *Succinct* – it conveys key information in a lively way using a few words

*Example 3: newsletter article*

Too many customer newsletters bore their readers with glowing prose about the company. This article starts from the readers' perspective. Instead of telling them how great the theme parks and leisure complexes are, it starts with a useful article full of ways of keeping children entertained during the long summer holiday. As part of the article the company quite reasonably promotes its wares, but it does not ram them down the reader's throat. They are merely presented as options. This soft-sell approach can work well in customer newsletters.

Now that you have sharpened your critical skills, apply them to your own work. Gather together copy you have produced in the past. Analyse and dissect it. Spot your weak points. See how you can improve it.

# 9 How the pros do it

Have you ever read great copy and wondered how on earth the copy-writer came up with such apt words, such stylish prose, such powerful copy? This chapter will take you inside the heads of some of Britain's top copywriters. Look at the copy they produce and find out how they approached the task and came up with the concept for their copy. You can also find out what their top tips are.

If you've ever wanted to write like a real pro, stop dreaming and start doing. Begin by learning from professional copywriters. Pay special attention to marketing copywriting – even when you are at home with a magazine, or watching TV. Analyse adverts, brochures and mail-shots. Try to work out what techniques are being used and to what effect. Pick up tips and ideas from other writers and adapt them to your needs. Remember that your aim is not to copy their style, simply to learn from it and to develop a style that is you.

In this chapter we will take a behind-the-scenes look at the work of professional copywriters. Read the copy they have written and find out how they arrived at the finished piece.

## Felicity Johnson: Disneyland Paris brochure

Felicity Johnson started her working life as a nurse, followed by five years' travelling and working in the Caribbean and at ski resorts. On her return to the UK she started work on a ski magazine. This led to a career in travel journalism, where she was published – among others – by *The Sunday Times*. In 1990 she co-founded the design consultancy Front Page, where as a director one of her main func-tions is copywriting. Other clients include marine engineers, tour operators, a management consultancy and a regional water authority. She has also worked on a variety of projects for The Walt Disney Company.

It was through these that Felicity was invited to write the copy in the Disneyland Paris brochure 1996/7. This was no mean feat: she got the brief for the brochure at the end of the week, flew out to Paris for three days at Disneyland, and completed the copy by the following week. To complicate matters, her text had to be suitable for translation into six other European languages (and still fit the same space in the brochure).

How did she move from a blank VDU screen to a finished 60-page brochure in less than a fortnight? 'I was helped,' explained Felicity, 'by a really comprehensive brief. Added to this, the design of the brochure was already complete, leaving me with the task of having to write text to fit a pre-defined space.' Felicity's approach was to write from a child's viewpoint in the hope of winning over doting parents. For example, she opens the brochure with:

> Laugh until your sides are sore, rub your eyes in sheer disbelief and pinch yourself to make sure you're not dreaming! Shake hands with Mickey Mouse, run into Goofy or chase Tigger. Join Peter Pan on his flight. See fairy tales come true and get swept into the joy of Christmas. Watch in wonder as the world lights up like magic and dream about doing it all over again tomorrow!

Felicity explained: 'It would have been impossible to write everything there is to say about Disneyland Paris, so I decided to concentrate on trying to encapsulate the emotions of a child on a visit to Disneyland. That involved going there myself, watching families and talking to children. I had to get the feel of the place first, experience the real magic.' During her visit, Felicity did not try to write copy, she simply took notes of anything that took her attention. These notes were purely factual, not creative. She also wrote down quotes from parents and children. Back at her desk she made use of the quotes, rewriting them to retain the gist while ensuring succinctness. 'People rarely talk in "soundbites" so editing quotes is essential.' She also took copious notes during her meeting with the Disneyland Paris marketing director. Many of the things he said about the place were developed by Felicity into snappy copy. For example, he told Felicity that even when the sun went down, there was still plenty to do at Disneyland. This was worked by Felicity into:

> When the sun goes down, Disney lights up.

The starting point for Felicity was to devise a theme to hold the brochure together. After considering various options she decided to run with a 'where in the world' theme. She planned to write 'Where in the world can you laugh until your sides are sore?' 'Where in the world can you shake hands with Mickey Mouse? ...' and so on. This was a bit laboured, so she retained the theme, but used it in a more subtle way. 'Getting the first paragraph cracked was the most difficult. Once I'd got that right, the rest just flowed.'

Felicity made use of many copywriting tricks to give her copy a lift. Alliteration, for example:

Live the Legend

Family Fantasia

Disney Detail

Minutes from the magic ...

Wander at will ...

and also rhyme:

Gasp, scream and dream

Stay and play the Disney way!

Don't be late for your holiday date!

Pay the easy way

Felicity explained: 'I didn't ever think "Right, now it's time for a bit of alliteration or a spot of rhyme", but I was aware that I was using these techniques. They were deliberate.'

Felicity's top tips for aspiring copywriters: 'Don't be frightened. Just write as you speak. And remember that readers often suffer from information overload: they don't want to plough through loads of text. It's so easy to overwrite, especially if you are worried about missing out something important. But don't give way to temptation. Keep it short and simple.'

# Hotel Cheyenne

### Wild West Adventure!

**Y**ee haw! You'll need to be quick on the draw to stay at this hotel! From your very first step onto the wooden sidewalk, you'll feel like you've walked straight onto a movie set. Pure escapism, pure pleasure, pure Disney!
• Enter the spirit of the Wild West.
• Toss for who gets to sleep in the top bunk! Each room has a double bed as well as bunks – getting the kids to bed has never been so easy!
• Economical prices for quality accommodation.

**Child's Play:**
These cowboys sure know how to enjoy themselves. As well as ponies to ride, there's the playground, games arcade, magic show, face painting and treasure hunts to work up a healthy appetite. Just as well there's a special children's menu to keep the little critters quiet!

(Activities are not supervised, vary depending on the day, and for some there may be an additional charge.)

Western-style rooms feature one double bed and one bunk bed.
Rooms for guests with disabilities.

Chuckwagon Cafe features a buffet or barbecue specialities.
Red Garter Saloon with live country music.

Themed shop.
Free shuttle to the Theme Park.

*Complete list of hotel amenities on page 37.*

## Dan McCurdy: Vauxhall Wintercare

Since graduating with a degree in advertising and marketing, Dan McCurdy has spent nearly twenty years working in radio advertising. Currently he works as Creative Services Manager for Radio Clyde, one of Britain's biggest commercial stations. He has written, recorded, produced or directed over 15 000 radio commercials for a vast array of clients – from cheese-makers and car dealerships to solicitors and funeral directors. Dan's productions have picked up awards for creativity in the London International and Independent Radio Awards, the New York Radio Awards and the Mobius Awards in Chicago.

Dan wrote and produced the following advert for Vauxhall Motors:

| | |
|---|---|
| *Sfx.* * | *Howling winds – not too obviously.* |
| *Mvo.* ** | *(sensibly pleading with a hint of sarcasm.)* And now a message for all Vauxhall drivers ..... Let me appeal to you, on behalf of your car. With Wintercare from Vauxhall, we check the thermostat, we check the water pump, the fan belt, we drain and refill the cooling system with Vauxhall approved anti-freeze, we check hoses, clips and radiator caps, and we guarantee it for 12 000 miles or until the end of April '96 by our Wintercare Warranty. We do all this for £29.95 including VAT. It's a **small** price to pay to help your car through a *difficult* time. So let me petition your obvious good nature. Get the complete winter check, peace of mind for your Vauxhall, before your car calls you a Scrooge. |
| Dealer tag. | Wintercare – from Anytown Motors, Anytown – or call Anytown 123 123 and get help. |

\* = sound effects
\*\* = male voiceover

Dan's brief was to get Vauxhall drivers to think about a winter service and to visit their local Vauxhall dealership to get one carried out. The ad therefore opens with a signal to get the target audience pricking up their ears: 'And now a message for all Vauxhall drivers.'

Dan opted for a straight announcement approach: 'I considered various treatments for this ad,' says Dan. 'Jack Frost, two voices, a couple talking in a broken-down car in the middle of winter ... but I dismissed them all fairly early on. It was clear to me that a straight announcement was the route to take, enabling me to pass on all the necessary information in just 50 seconds.'

Dan chose to list many of the items covered by the winter check to show what good value the service was: 'In a way, what was included in the list was unimportant. What mattered was giving listeners the impression that they would get a comprehensive check covering all manner of things. By producing an impressive list, listeners are persuaded of the value.'

'The thing about radio scripts,' explains Dan, 'is that they look really dull on paper. That's because they are written to be heard, not read. Sound effects and a good voiceover really bring it to life. It's the spoken word that counts, not the written one.'

As for Dan's top tip: 'Remember who you are talking to.'

## Adrian Jeffery

From boyhood, Adrian Jeffery wanted to work in advertising. After school, he took a foundation course in art and design, followed by a degree in advertising. After working as a copywriter for various London and Edinburgh ad agencies he formed his own agency in 1994, with two other partners. He handles business for a number of high-profile clients, including Mother's Pride, Direct Line Insurance, Opto Eyecare and Drambuie liqueur.

Adrian's ads, a series of four for a bed-and-breakfast establishment, are certainly different from the average B&B ads one comes across. Adrian explained why he adopted this novel approach: 'The adverts were to be placed in one publication only – *The Drum*. This is a specialist publication for people working in advertising and the media. Its readers are more style-conscious and they have a higher threshold for controversy and even for insults. We knew that we had to be more arresting in order to attract attention, but also that we could push boundaries a little further. We would never have taken this approach for ads designed to appear in a mainstream publication.'

As someone involved in advertising, Adrian had a very clear image of who he was writing for: people like himself. But he also had to get to know the product he was advertising, and to know his client. First step was to see the owner at the B&B, to talk, to look around, and to really understand what he was selling. 'Fortunately the owner had a very clear view of where he wanted to position his product: upmarket. At the same time, he did not want to come across as pompous or stuffy, like some upmarket establishments. His proposition was twofold. He was offering something as good as a hotel, but not as expensive. And he was offering a guesthouse that suffered none of the unpleasant features of other guesthouses.'

Once Adrian had a clear understanding of what was on offer and what his client wanted to achieve through the ads, it was time to get started on the creative side. He sat down with his art director and brainstormed all of the awful features of the average boarding house – such as shared bathrooms and nylon sheets. These, of course, are the things that are definitely not on offer at the Acorn Lodge. Having decided that the bad features would make arresting headlines, he decided that that was exactly what he should do: turn them into headlines. At first glance it would look as if they related to the Acorn Lodge, yet the reader would know that no advertiser would allow such negative copy to be written about them. Obviously readers would need to look beyond the headline to find its meaning. Having got the reader hooked, Adrian was free to use the body copy to really sell the Acorn Lodge.

'We split the ads into two groups,' explained Adrian. 'Two of the ads have a go at hotels, while the other two knock B&Bs. Having knocked out the opposition we are free to focus on the benefits of our client.'

The challenge for Adrian was coming up with an idea for the series of ads: 'Getting the concept right was the key. Once that was clear, writing the ads was relatively easy. All we had to do was follow the formula we had established. Having said that, I drafted the body copy for each ad several times before it was right. I was trying to build up a mental picture of the place, one that would change people's prejudices about B&Bs. That meant conjuring up a rich image. For example, I deliberately wrote about "Irish linen" rather than just "linen". It sounded superior and helped position the place.'

The tone of voice of the ads was also important to Adrian. 'I wanted a style that was easy to read,' he said. 'My aim was to lead the reader from sentence to sentence, trying to keep them interested and entertained. Given that the ads were so small, the real challenge was keeping it all short and succinct, while at the same time creating a feeling that the Acorn Lodge is a great place.'

Knowing he was producing a campaign of ads, Adrian deliberately stuck to one point per advert. 'Too many ads try to say too much. I concentrated on one selling point per ad, knowing that readers would recognize the ads as being from the same stable and read the other ads in the series.'

Adrian's advice for aspiring copywriters is to spend plenty of time researching the product. 'I was commissioned to produce a press

£7.95 for snotty eggs and fatty bacon

is a total rip off, not to mention a disgusting way to start the day. That's why when you stay at The Acorn Lodge we make sure that breakfast is really worth getting up for. Choices include Eggs Benedict, Vegetarian, the full Scottish breakfast of course and a themed "Breakfast of the week". All cooked freshly to order. And all fully inclusive in the room price.

**ACORN LODGE** GUEST HOUSE
26 Pilrig Street, Edinburgh EH6 5AJ.
Tel: 0131 555 1557. e-mail:acorn@ednet.co.uk
Prices: £25-£40 per person per night B&B.

advert for the oriental rug department of a big store. I spent a long time interviewing the rug buyer, finding out about the rugs on sale, and even reading up on Persian carpets. If you make an effort at the research stage you will find it so much easier to get started when you get down to writing.'

So now you know how the professionals do it. Although each of the copywriters featured has their own distinctive style, they share a similar approach. Each spends time getting to know and understand the product. None of them sits down and writes copy straight off. All

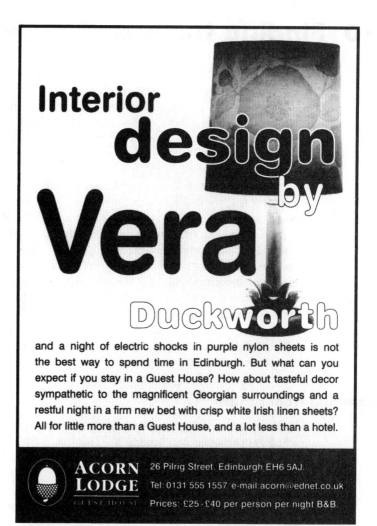

**Interior design by Vera Duckworth**

and a night of electric shocks in purple nylon sheets is not the best way to spend time in Edinburgh. But what can you expect if you stay in a Guest House? How about tasteful decor sympathetic to the magnificent Georgian surroundings and a restful night in a firm new bed with crisp white Irish linen sheets? All for little more than a Guest House, and a lot less than a hotel.

**ACORN LODGE** GUEST HOUSE

26 Pilrig Street, Edinburgh EH6 5AJ.
Tel: 0131 555 1557. e-mail:acorn@ednet.co.uk
Prices: £25 - £40 per person per night B&B.

of them make use of the various devices available to copywriters. It is clear that a shared approach need not result in a samey style. Techniques can help you get the job done, without standing in the way of your personal style.

# 10 Finding the creative you

Inside every marketing and business person there is a creative writer waiting to get out. Find out in this chapter how to unlock the creative you and where to look for inspiration. Have a go with different writing styles, using a series of exercises designed to develop your creativity.

I always thought the term 'creative accountancy' (the polite term for 'cooking the books') was a curious one. Of all professions, accountancy must be the one least prone to creativity. So, if that most staid of professions can find creativity within them, so can you.

Children are amazingly creative people. They draw and paint, build models, play act, even make up new words. Sadly this innate creativity dries up with age. Or rather, we become self-conscious and inhibited. By the time we reach adulthood many of us have forgotten how to be creative any more. Thankfully we can restore our creativity, and the exercises at the end of this chapter will help do just that. Other ways of boosting creativity include the following.

## Learning from others

In the previous chapter you read how various professional copywriters approached an assignment. Think how they went about it and see if you can take a similar approach. You will probably find that you cannot take an 'approach to creativity' off-the-shelf. You will need to tailor it to fit you and your own way of working. You must find your own approach, but you can do this by adjusting the way others work so that you are comfortable with it.

Another idea, covered in Chapter 8, is to analyse others' copy. Look at press ads, leaflets and other marketing material. See if you can work out how the copywriter arrived at the finished item. Try to map out the process involved. See if those steps could be applied by you when you have a new assignment.

Sometimes creativity comes from within. A brilliant idea emerges from you unprompted. At other times you might find that you need a catalyst. Some people can come up with great ideas, but not cold. They need something to spark an idea or to get them in the right mood. They need to find a way to open their mind.

## Inspiration and ideas

I have an 'inspiration box' which acts as my catalyst. It's just a cardboard box, but it's filled with material that has inspired me – press ads, leaflets, annual reports, posters, cards, direct mail packages, indeed anything at all that I have been impressed by. On days when I am not feeling very inspired, I simply reach for my cardboard box and delve in. Soon my mind is buzzing with ideas. Remember that the idea of an inspiration box is not to plagiarize but to prompt.

I also have an ideas box. This shoe box differs from my inspiration box in that it contains my own ideas. Whenever I have an idea, however crazy, I write it down on a small piece of paper, which is then stored in the shoe box. When I'm in need of a good idea, I tip the contents of the shoe box on my desk and see what's there. Sometimes I can lift an idea direct, or I may have to adapt it. I frequently find that the ideas act as catalysts for new, unrelated ideas.

A variation on my ideas box, some people force themselves to come up with a thought or idea each day. The crazier and less inhibited, the better. These thoughts, ideas and observations are pinned up around their office, and colleagues and visitors are invited to add to them.

## Word games

Some copywriters play word games to warm themselves up and get their creative juices flowing. They might, for example, invent collective nouns or amusing spoonerisms.

## The writing on the wall

Some of the best lines I have read have appeared not in slick advertising but on the walls of public lavatories. Putting aside the less salubrious offerings, there are some real gems. But even the risqué can be amusing, such as this from a gents' loo back in the 1960s (before fur became unacceptable): One boastful man had written: 'I've got something every woman wants' to which the ultimate put-down was added: 'You must be in the fur coat business.' It seems to me that if men can write readable copy on the lavvy, then anyone can be a copywriter! But seriously, graffiti can be really creative, particularly the way it grows as people add to it.

## Getting your surroundings right

Environment is important for a copywriter. I pity you if you are expected to produce creative copy from a desk in a busy, open plan, strip-lit office. I prefer soft lighting, peace and no interruptions to interrupt my flow. Busy managers might find this notion a little self-indulgent, but who cares? Writing is as much an art as a craft, and writers need the right environment to stimulate their creative urges. So if at all possible, create a workspace for yourself that will nurture your creativity, not strangle it. It is said that the great French novelist Honoré de Balzac would not write unless he had an unripe apple on his desk! Many writers have their foibles. They may be famous authors, while you are just a humble wannabe copywriter. But that's not to say that you cannot afford yourself the same indulgences. After all, the big names were once small ones. But don't take it too far. You can succumb a little to artistic temperament, but always maintain a businesslike discipline that ensures you get the job done. Try the ideas outlined above and see how your creativity grows.

They say that practice makes perfect. Certainly practice will help you to improve your writing: the more you write, the better you will get. The problem is that most people hate writing and would rather avoid it than practise it. If you genuinely want to be a good copywriter, there is no alternative but to practise. The best way to start is to work through the following exercises, which have been designed to build creativity.

## Eleven exercises to build creativity

Work through these exercises in any order you like. Don't be put off by any that prove difficult. It's only by taxing yourself that you will improve your writing skills. For each completed exercise, write it up and place it in a ringbinder. Whenever you feel your confidence waning, pull out your ringbinder and remind yourself of the wide range of writing assignments you have tackled.

*Exercise 1*

**Assignment**
Write a twelve-page children's book. You must write a complete story that will appeal to the average four-year-old. Use language appropriate for the age group. Do not exceed 600 words. The final book will be illustrated. Indicate clearly what text and what illustrations will be on each page. Ensure each illustration complements the words.

## What you will learn

> - How to use a different writing style
> - How to write for a well-defined audience with very particular needs
> - How to use appropriate language
> - How to get words and pictures working in harmony (see the next chapter for more information on this)
> - How to get a lot of information across in a lively manner using just a few words

*Exercise 2*

### Assignment

Think of fifteen suitable yet appealing adjectives to describe each of the following products:

> - Expensive perfume
> - Cheap baked beans
> - An exclusive brand of caviar
> - An affordable 'run-around' hatchback car
> - A top of the range Jaguar car
> - A girl's doll
> - A boy's doll – Action Man or similar
> - An office swivel typists' chair
> - A new machine for making nuts and bolts
> - A multi-media personal computer

### What you will learn

If you are having difficulty writing a piece of copy, it can sometimes be useful to start by listing suitable adjectives, as a warm-up to get you in the right frame of mind. It can also spark an idea which you can develop when you come to writing your copy. This exercise, by asking for fifteen adjectives, should tax your wordpower to its limit.

*Exercise 3*

### Assignment

Complete the following exercise without a thesaurus. Think of as many synonyms as possible for each of the following words:

- Children
- Box
- Money
- Exhibition
- Seat
- Happy
- Empty
- End

## What you will learn

A mistake frequently made by amateur copywriters is word repetition. The challenge for copywriters is to come up with different ways of saying the same thing, and that's where synonyms come in. You need to be skilled at using synonyms and should always have a thesaurus at your side when you work. (Many software programs incorporate a thesaurus, but these are not as comprehensive as their paper equivalents.) When you are writing and there is a risk of repetition, list the words you will need to repeat and then come up with alternatives. Select from your list of alternatives when you start to write.

*Exercise 4*

## Assignment

Here is a completed crossword. Come up with cryptic clues for each of the answers.

| $H_1$ | E | L | $L_2$ | O |
|-------|---|---|-------|---|
| A | ■ | | O | ■ |
| $L_3$ | E | $M_4$ | O | $N_5$ |
| I | ■ | I | ■ | I |
| B | ■ | N | ■ | C |
| $U_6$ | $N_7$ | C | L | E |
| $T_8$ | O | E | ■ | |

| Across | Down |
|--------|------|
| 1 | 1 |
| 3 | 2 |
| 6 | 4 |
| 8 | 5 |
| | 7 |

**What you will learn**

By having to provide definitions to everyday words you will learn how to be precise and clear with language. You will also learn how to play with words.

*Exercise 5*

**Assignment**

Have you ever looked through old newspapers and magazines and smiled at the outmoded adverts? Even ads from the 1960s and 1970s look outdated, let alone those from the 1900s or 1920s.

Imagine you are working on a press advert for washing powder. Step into a time machine and speed back to the 1920s. Write an ad in an appropriate style for the period. Then do one for the same washing powder, but this time in a 1960s style. Finally, write the sort of ad that might be used today. Write the copy and indicate where visuals/graphics will go and what they will show.

**What you will learn**

Sometimes advertisers use a 'period' style advert. Because it looks or sounds so different, it stands out from the contemporary and attracts attention, which is the first adage of advertising (AIDA – the acronym for attention, interest, desire and action). You can use a period feel for other material too, such as newsletters and annual reports. Let's say you were celebrating your company's centenary. A customer newsletter produced with sepia-tinted photos, genuine company ads from the 1880s, and text written in a Victorian style could be a great and memorable gimmick. A psychedelic annual report to celebrate the anniversary of a company founded in the Swinging Sixties, with lots of fab, groovy and 'far out' copy, would have the same effect.

*Exercise 6*

**Assignment: Part 1**

Imagine you are working for a dog food manufacturer called Bonzo. Write a short press ad for the product that features rhyme.

**Assignment: Part 2**

Now write a slogan for the same dog food, this time using alliteration.

**What you will learn**

Rhyme can be used to good effect in marketing copy. Remember the 'Lipsmakin' thirstquenchin' ...' Pepsi advert from the 1970s?

I remember people trying to learn the words, and others wearing T-shirts with the rhyme printed across. It can be difficult to use rhyme well, so practise as much as you can.

Slogans, too, are powerful marketing tools, and writing them is an art. They require to be memorable, meaningful, snappy and apt. If you would like to look over a massive collection of slogans, consult *Slogans* (edited by Laurence Urdang and Ceila Dame Robbins, Gale Research Company, 1984). It is a collection of over 6000 slogans used in advertising, political campaigns, etc. arranged by thematic categories such as aerospace, shampoo, coffee and furniture.

*Exercise 7*

**Assignment: Part 1**
Think up three suitable product names for each of the following:

> - A range of luxury catfood whose recipes were devised by top chef Anton Mossiman
> - A new over-the-counter drug to reduce flatulence
> - A lightweight mobile crane for use on building sites

**Assignment: Part 2**
Here are two products:

> - A nippy little hatchback car that's perfect for city driving
> - A luxury executive car with leather seats and walnut dashboard

Here are two product names:

> - The Churchill
> - The Zipper

Assign each of the products with the relevant product name. Write an explanation of why you chose which name for which product.

**What you will learn**
Some companies spend thousands, tens or even hundreds of thousands of pounds on developing the right product names. Clearly some words have strong connotations and are chosen for this reason. This exercise gets you to think about the hidden meaning of words and how a simple word can conjure up so much more, adding subtle meaning to a product.

*Exercise 8*

**Assignment**
I read my first limerick, aged six, in my *Basil Brush Annual*. It went something like this:

This was a young woman from Twickenham
Whose shoes were too tight to walk quick in 'em
Once, after a walk
Looking whiter than chalk
She took 'em both off and got sick in 'em

Write an amusing limerick about a copywriter.

**What you will learn**
Copywriters need to be able to turn their hand to anything. While most of your work is straight prose, there may be times when you have to adopt a very different, even gimmicky, style. This exercise will show you that you can do the most silly assignment with aplomb!

*Exercise 9*

**Assignment**
I once heard a radio programme in which listeners were asked to come up with a collective noun for smokers who huddle outside their smoke-free offices for a sly ciggie. My two favourites were cigeratti and fagarazzi. See if you can come up with three of your own.

**What you will learn**
This exercise will get you to think about language in a creative way. Sometimes marketing copy requires words to be invented and this exercise will give you experience of the technique.

*Exercise 10*

**Assignment**
This assignment builds upon the previous one. My toddler is great at making up words. They're not nonsense words, they are invented words that are apt and their meaning immediately clear. For example, when he soaks me with his water pistol, he says he is 'schooshing' me. It's a wonderfully onomatopoeic word. Living in Edinburgh, he's familiar with the bone-shaking feeling of being pushed across cobblestones in his pushchair. When he travels downstairs on his bottom, he calls it 'cobbling' because the effect is similar. This linguistic creativity shown by young children is lost

when we become self-conscious adults. Revive it by making up some words of your own. Come up with at least five new words, along with definitions.

**What you will learn**
Sometimes memorable copy uses made-up words. Adverts for Smint mints use the made-up word 'sminted' as a verb in their slogan 'Have you been sminted?'. Whiskas cat food talk about 'catisfaction'. You might find that a made-up word can help your company get noticed.

*Exercise 11*

**Assignment: Part 1**
Imagine you have just opened a portion of delicious chip shop chips, wrapped in newspaper, and generously sprinkled with salt and vinegar. Describe how they:

- Look – their appearance, colour
- Smell
- Taste
- Feel

Be as descriptive and evocative as you can.

**Assignment: Part 2**
Now repeat the exercise, but substitute the chips with one of your company's products. Ignore any of the senses that do not apply, and add sound to the list, if appropriate.

**What you will learn**
Your ability to successfully promote your products through your marketing material will be dependent to a large extent on your powers of description. This is particularly important where you are selling holidays and other experiences – though it could be argued that the senses come into play for all products.

Here's how you can use the power of the senses to write copy that has more punch.

✔ A deserted tropical beach bright with golden moonlight. Sea lapping over coral. Warm breezes sending wafts of jasmine and ylang ylang. This is Bariba, the most beautiful Caribbean island ever.

The above passage involves the reader. It takes them to the island and lets them experience the sights, sounds and smells. Compare it with this:

> ✗ Bariba Island is a Caribbean island that offers peace and tranquillity for those seeking a holiday away from the cut and thrust of city life.

Something's lacking in this version – the sensations.

If you have managed to work through these exercises, you will have gained experience of a wide range of copywriting assignments that will help you increase your wordsmithing skills. Why not put your work to one side, then repeat the exercises again in a month or two's time? Compare the two and see how your skill keeps developing.

# 11 Making words work in harmony with design

Whether it is a press advert or a sales brochure, most of what you write will be professionally designed. This chapter will explain how to work with graphic designers to produce text that works in harmony with design. You can also pick up tips on how to write the sort of copy that looks good (as well as reads well) on the printed page.

Choosing and using the right words is what copywriting is all about. But good copy takes more than just a few well-chosen words. Most marketing material is a combination of words and pictures/designed images. How well these words and pictures work together can be the deciding factor in how effective the material is. Great words presented through lousy design will result in inferior marketing material. To get your words working at full capacity you need to ensure that they are teamed up with first-rate design. Design needs to:

- Make the most of the words
- Add something extra to the words
- Enhance the words by working in harmony with them

Text that ignores design, or design that ignores text, is doomed. So as a copywriter you need to be design-aware. You must understand the part design can play in marketing material, you need to be aware of devices you can use to get copy and design working together, and you need to have design firmly in your mind as you write your copy. The best marketing material is produced by copywriters working in partnership with designers. If you write copy without regard to design, you can't expect the two to work in harmony and, if they don't, you won't have such powerful marketing material.

Writing with an eye to design is not difficult. You don't have to be both a designer and a wordsmith, but you do need to be able to think in words and in pictures. You need to bear in mind how design can:

- Give the necessary prominence and impact to key words, sentences or paragraphs on the page

- Give the right emphasis to each part of your writing
- Draw attention to the most important parts
- Make your text as easy as possible to read
- Provide meaning or emotion more powerfully than words

Sometimes it is impossible to write copy until you have an image of the finished design in your head. Take the following examples:

In this advert for a car fitted with a device to warn of any traffic jams in a 10-mile radius, the headline reads:

Rapid Relief from the Misery of Congestion

The photo (the main focus of the advert) shows a picture of cars bumper to bumper in a mega traffic snarl-up. The headline on its own could refer to a flu remedy; the accompanying photograph gives new meaning to the headline and causes a laugh. Without the mental picture of a traffic jam, the copywriter would not have come up with this headline. Here's another advert along similar lines, again for a car:

Avoid painful fillings

This advert shows a car alongside a petrol pump. The body copy explains how fuel efficient the car is. Who would come up with a headline like this unless they had design in mind? By thinking visually as well as verbally you open doors to creativity. You give yourself the opportunity to let pictures speak for you, or to provide fodder for clever headlines and puns. If you cannot think visually you cut yourself off from all of this, leaving your work potentially flat and one-dimensional.

## Making the most of words

Words can (and, where appropriate, should) work in partnership with pictures. But design need not rely on pictures; sometimes it can be used to make the most of words on their own. Linguists use the term 'graphology' to describe how words look. Copywriters and designers can use a variety of graphological devices to draw attention to words, giving them added power and meaning. Here are some of the many copywriting and design devices you can use to make the most of your words:

### 1 Repeated letters

In radio and TV ads, repeated sounds can be used to attract attention. In print you can get the same effect by repeating letters. You can emphasize particular letters by:

● *Enlargement* – let's say you were writing an ad to promote a luxurious cruise on the *SS Steamer*. You might write:

> **SS**uperior **SS**pecial **SS**umptuous
> **SS**ail with the *SS SSteamer*

Your designer could produce artwork showing the 'SS' letters in the same colours and logotype as the *SS Steamer*, thus visually reinforcing the written message.

● *Capitalization* – a company wanted to show its expertise in information technology (IT), so it commissioned a series of ads which featured the benefits it offered. Each showed a one-word benefit in which the letters 'IT' appeared in upper case, such as productiv**IT**y, followed by a strapline. By capitalizing the key letters it was possible to get across two messages using just one word. A garage offering MOTs could use the same device:

> **MOT**orist **MOT**orway
> Get in **MOT**ion
> Get your **MOT** at **MOT**ability

● *One letter, several slots* – sometimes you can take a letter and, through careful layout, get that one letter to fill several slots. For example:

> Tobin's Teacakes
> Put the T into Teatime
>
> TastiesTobin's
> e
> a
> c
> a
> k
> e
> s

This example works at a number of levels. The slogan, Put the Tea into Teatime, is reinforced by the use of the letter T, which is reproduced in the same font. The shape made by the words is T-shaped. It's not wonderful copy when read out loud, but as a designed advert it is effective.

### 2 Uncommon letters

Another graphological technique is to use uncommon letters to draw attention to your copy. As you skim-read copy, uncommon letters leap out – X, Q, Z, J and K, for example. The less common letters are those which tend to attract the higher scores in the word game *Scrabble*. (E is the most common letter in English, followed by T, A, I and S.) For obvious reasons, it can be tricky to write copy that uses uncommon letters. One way to use them is spell ordinary words in a different way: stax rather than stacks, loox not looks, cheez not cheese. Such words sound the same (and, therefore, are not suitable for radio advertising) but look different and are therefore ideal for written copy.

If you were advertising a brand of cheese called Cheezz, you could use the Z to full effect like this:

---

If your cheese is boring ... *z z z z z z z z*

Try our Cheezz

---

Here the Z is used to suggest snoring, reinforcing the dullness of other cheeses.

Of these uncommon letters, it would appear that 'X' is the most popular. I did a one-minute brainstorm of product names and came up with the following: Dettox, Pipex, Dulux, Tippex, Kleenex, Rolex, Durex, Radox, Biotex, Copydex, OXO, Sandtex, Moulinex, Exlax and Zovirax. No doubt you'll be able to add to the list.

Famously, Heinz uses this technique with its 'Beanz Meanz Heinz' slogan. When read aloud, the slogan features rhyme and assonance. When seen in print, repetition (of the letter 'Z') plus the use of an unusual letter (Z) and unusual spelling (beanz meanz) attracts attention.

You have to be careful with this technique. Some have used it in a cringe-inducing way. How often have you seen shops called Krazy Kutz or Kwik something or other? Unless you want your product to appear naff and downmarket, try to be a bit more original.

### 3 Onomatopoeia

Another useful technique is to change the spelling of a word so that it becomes onomatopoeic. Panasonic's hiss-free cordless phone was advertised like this:

> Introducing a cordless telephone with something missssing

### 4 Splitting words

A word technique that relies on design for its effect is the practice of breaking or splitting a word or words into new combinations. Take, for example, this advert for low-fat sunflower margarine:

> SUNF
>     LOWER

You need to look twice to work it out. When you do, you see that it's a sunflower spread that is lower in fat. It's clever because it says a lot in just one word, and it engages the reader in interpreting its meaning.

Here's another example, also for a spread, which uses the technique in a different way. This billboard advert shows butter melting over a close-up shot of corn on the cob. The text says:

> All you need is love

On closer inspection you see that what it actually says is:

> All you need is clover

The 'c' and 'r' in 'clover' (the brand name for the product) are printed in green; all the rest of the text is in yellow. It is the design which gives this double meaning, but it is the copywriter who produced the wording which could be designed to create this effect.

Essentially this is a visual pun. There are many examples of visual puns in marketing material. Perhaps most famous for their puns are Perrier, the French mineral water manufacturer. They produced an amazingly large and funny range of adverts which used 'eau' (the French word for water, pronounced 'o') in place of the letter 'O' in a variety of words. They showed, for example, a bottle of Perrier with the headline:

H₂Eau

In another ad they showed a modern art, cubist-style painting of a bottle of Perrier with the headline:

Picasseau

These adverts were clever because:

- Copy and design worked together
- The use of the French word 'eau' reinforced the French origin of the drink
- The 'eau' punning was apt, since it was promoting water
- The 'eau' sound gave the ads a French accent
- Overall this produced witty, appealing and memorable adverts

*5 Symbols as letters or words*

Sometimes you can use a relevant symbol in place of a letter. For example:

SAVE MON£Y AT ZIGGY'S

I L♥VE HEARTS BISTRO

D■N'T BE SQUARE WHEN IT C■MES TO FASHI■N –
GET R●UND TO SP●●K'S B●UTIQUE N●W

Symbols have instant meaning for us. By using a symbol in place of a letter we can reinforce our point. We can also use symbols to replace words.

*6 Letters as words or sentences*

You can also use letters on their own to signify a word. Lucozade ran a campaign around the letters NRG (energy). You could have:
XTC (ecstasy)
MT (empty)
XL (excel)
See what words and sentences you can make up! British Telecom (BT) used this technique in reverse with its Beattie (BT) character, played by Maureen Lipman.

### 7 Letters and numbers

You can also mix numbers with letters to form words. Take this ludicrous example which I made up to illustrate the technique. It is for a fictitious company called 10-10 Tenders:

> When it comes to 10-ders we have the 10-acity of a K9. Heaven 4-bid that anyone should undercut us on price. So if you want a competitive quote, call **10-10 Tenders**.

### 8 Homophones

A homophone is a word that sounds the same as another but has a different meaning (and often a different spelling too). For example, place/plaice, gays/gaze, staid/stayed, a frayed knot/afraid not. Many puns are based on homophones and, for obvious reasons, they work better in print than when spoken. Here are two of my favourites:

A car sticker for a Christian organization:

> 7 days without prayer makes one weak

An advert showing a photo of a Scottish lake:

> Sainsbury's have discovered that the finest whisky is kept under loch and quay

### 9 Writing in a shape

This is a technique that you might have used at school. Your text forms a shape which is related to the subject you are writing about. Let's say you were producing a brochure for a garden supplier. Your text could be set out in the shape of a tree, a flower, a watering can and so on. British Airways used this technique in press ads to publicize their new reclinable seats. Text describing other airlines' seats was laid out to look like an uncomfortable, rather upright seat. Text describing their recliners was laid out to resemble a reclining seat. By setting the text to form a shape, the message of the words was reinforced visually.

## Good copy and good design: bedfellows for great marketing material

As you can see from the above examples, words used in combination with design and layout produce more powerful marketing material. Good communication frequently relies on words and pictures working together. So do not regard design as something additional to words, but as something integral to them. Good design and layout can really bring copy to life and give it an added dimension. Copy that may look rather flat and lifeless on a VDU screen or on sheets of white A4 paper can be skilfully brought to life through clever typography and design. If you want to communicate your message effectively, you must write it well. Good design will not transform bad copy into good copy. Equally, good copy will be done no justice by bad design. Each must complement the other.

## When to give more emphasis to design than copy

For some marketing assignments photos and illustrations will need to be given more emphasis than the text. This is particularly important where the assignment is focusing on style and image, or where a product is differentiated by its appearance (fashion clothes or cars, for example). It is also the case where a product is difficult to write about, such as perfume. Here, glamorous or romantic images take the place of text. And, of course, images should always be used in place of copy if the chosen picture really can, as the saying goes, do the job of a thousand words. A photo of a child, face alight with delight as he opens his birthday presents, is probably far more compelling than a verbal description of that scene. It can convey the emotion more quickly, more powerfully and more effectively than words could. The same can be said for diagrams and their ability to show complex information in a clear, simple and easy to understand way. Imagine trying to explain the layout of the London Underground in words!

## Working with designers

To get the best out of a designer you need to let them into your head. Explain as much as you can about your copy – who it is for, what points you are trying to convey, which are the key parts. Tell them what kind of an image you are trying to create – upmarket, trendy, sophisticated, informal. Make sure they understand what you are trying to achieve. Once they are fully briefed, hand over the copy, but only after you have given it a thorough check.

Before giving copy to a designer, print out your work and read through it very carefully. Check:

- Spelling
- Punctuation
- For typos

## Different kinds of typo

Typos (typographical errors) can spoil otherwise good copy and talented design. Essentially there are three types of typo:

- *The finger slip* – this is where your fingers slip on the keyboard, so instead of typing 'son' you type 'aon'. (The 'S' key is next to the 'A' key so typos like this are easily made.) Thankfully they are as easy to spot as they are to make, and they can be picked up with ease by your word processor's spellchecking software. You will probably find that you have a handful of typos of this sort that you keep making. My own most common typo is 'thge' instead of 'the'.
- *The concentration lapse* – tired and distracted copywriters make mistakes. All it takes is a short concentration lapse and you'll find that errors have crept in. You might, for example, type 'be' for 'by', 'you' for 'your' or 'is' for 'in'. This kind of typo can be a devil to spot. Your spellchecker will miss them, since they are proper (albeit the wrong) words. Chances are that you, too, will overlook them. You see, we tend to read what we think is there, not what is actually there. (I was determined that my first book would have no typos in it, and I took great care to read and reread the page proofs, and to get others to do it too. But yes, you've guessed it – after publication I spotted three.)
- *Editing typos* – these typos arise when you move text about. Let's say you remove a wodge of text then add in a new bit. You might find that you have left a straggling word behind that should have been removed. Or you change one part of the sentence and forget to change the rest to make sense.

## Top tips for spotting typos

- Print out your copy before proofing, as it is easier to spot the mistakes on paper than on a VDU screen

- Get someone else to proof your copy too
- Read text aloud
- Read the page from bottom to top, and even right to left, to read what's actually there (as opposed to what you expect to see there)

## Checking what comes back

Hand over perfect text to your designer, and check just as carefully what you get back. Errors often creep in at design stage. You might find, on seeing your copy designed, that you want to revisit the text to make some edits aimed at enhancing the design. For example, you might find that your copy is slightly too long (by just two or three words), forcing your designer to start a new page. It helps in such cases if text can be edited to help it fit the allocated space. Sometimes you can gain a whole line by deleting or shortening just one word.

Look over the designed proofs and check that the designer has given the right prominence to your words. Perhaps they have emphasized a section of text that is not all that important, or ignored one that is. Maybe they have treated your subheads as main headings. Check everything and make sure it is correct.

# PART 2

This part explains how to approach the main pieces of work you are likely to have to produce – from news releases and newsletters to direct mail and adverts. Each chapter shows step by step how to do it, with helpful tips and advice.

# 12 A direct mail package

This chapter looks at the complete direct mail package, starting with the envelope and going through to the covering letter and any enclosures. Find out step by step how to produce powerful packages to help you sell through the letterbox.

Direct mail acquired the derisory term 'junk mail' because much of it was (and sometimes still is) badly targeted and poorly written. Since our subject is copywriting, not marketing, we will stick to the copy aspect of direct mail. But remember that wonderful words will fail to sell if you send them to the wrong people. Good copywriting is a partner in successful direct mail, effective only if combined with accurate targeting.

There are three steps a reader will take if you have produced a well put together, tightly targeted mailshot:

1   They will look at and then open the envelope
2   They will read the contents
3   They will place an order (or take some other desired action)

The steps are taken in that order; a reader will not place an order unless they have first opened the envelope and read the mailing. Your task as copywriter, then, is to get the envelope opened. We all open our personal mail: indeed, we look forward to receiving it. A pastel-pink envelope bearing cousin Susan's distinctive handwriting will probably be opened, and eagerly read. But a pile of unsolicited 'junk' mail? That's another matter!

When you receive mailshots, whatever tricks the sender uses – such as mock handwriting, or personalization – you know that it's nothing more than a computer-generated mailing that is being sent to thousands or millions of others too. What do you do with it? Bin it unopened? Take a quick look and then bin it? Or keenly tear it open, read all the contents, and place an order straight away? How your reader reacts is down to you – and the care you have taken with the package.

## The envelope

I will start by looking at the outside of your mailshot: the envelope. This is what is first seen by the recipient. If it's not right, your prospect will not open it. If they don't open it, they can't read its contents and can't place an order. Your hard work will be consigned to the waste paper basket. That's why you need to think of the envelope not just as a carrier for your mailing but as an integral part of the package. It can make the difference between a mailing being opened or being binned. It's that important.

You can, if you wish, use plain white or manila envelopes for mailshots. Alternatively, you can have envelopes made for you and printed with your message. If you are going for the printed option, you need to think carefully about the envelope's copy and design. Deciding on this is every bit as important a copywriting task as writing the enclosures.

Most printed envelopes carry a message designed to attract the reader and get them to open the mailing. There are three approaches you can take:

---

- *Urgent* – urgency works in marketing copy because it encourages action. Use words likely to create a sense of urgency, such as: 'Open **now** to save £600' or 'We've got great offers inside, but **hurry** – stocks are limited'.
- *Teasing* – envelope teasers can capture the imagination of the recipient and encourage them to open the mailing. You might, for example, write on the envelope: 'A singing dog'. This cryptic message could be bizarre enough to get your reader reaching for their letter opener.
- *Incomplete* – start a sentence on the envelope and complete it in the headline of your enclosure. Your aim is to use the envelope to get the reader reading your letter. Your envelope might say: 'The holiday of your dreams ...' and the covering letter continue with '... is yours for just £5 a week.' (Do not use this technique for business mailings: a secretary might open mail and discard envelopes before passing the contents on to the addressee.)

---

You can also use envelope messages to convey information:

---

- *Informative* – an informative statement printed on an envelope enables you to get a message across even if the envelope is never opened, e.g. a slogan such as 'Birmingham's Number One Gents' Outfitter' printed boldly across an envelope, along with a logo and address, could influence the recipient at some later date, even if they fail to open this particular mailing. It's important awareness-building.

---

Remember that any message on the envelope must link with the covering letter. For example, if your envelope says:

> 'Bald? We can restore your hair!'

then the headline of your covering letter should say:

> One Hirsute Pill each day transforms bald heads into crowning glories.

If you produce a successful envelope, you are over the first hurdle: getting the mailing opened. Obstacle number two is getting it read. Follow the advice here and you'll have a head-start.

## The enclosures

Most mailings comprise a covering letter and one enclosure. The enclosure may be:

- A mail order catalogue*
- An order form
- A reply card*
- A leaflet*
- A questionnaire
- A newsletter*
- A product sample
- A brochure
- A money-off voucher
- A pre-paid envelope

\* You can read more about these elsewhere in this book.

Whatever other enclosures are contained in your mailing, at least one is likely to be the covering letter.

## The covering letter

The covering letter is so important. If there are other enclosures, it acts as navigator, explaining to your readers what else is enclosed and why. It guides them through the mailing and leads them to take the necessary action. If the only enclosure is the letter, it becomes more important still. This is your one chance. There's no glossy brochure or free sample to back you up.

Your aim is to use the covering letter to capture the recipient's interest – immediately. If you fail to engage them straight away, you're done for. They will not read on in the hope of finding something interesting a few paragraphs later. No. They will give up. Goodbye order, hello dustbin.

Before starting on the covering letter, decide on its purpose. It will be one of four types:

> • *Sales* – these are letters that are designed to sell there and then (by getting the recipient to place an order)
> • *Lead-generating* – unlike sales letters, these letters aim to get the recipient to express an interest. You then follow up with a further mailing, phone call or a visit
> • *Information* – you might, for example, be writing to inform customers about price increases or changes to your service
> • *Navigational* – this type of letter steers your reader through the mailing, summarizing what's in it and what's on offer. Navigational letters can also be information, sales or lead-generating letters

## Sales letters

The writers of some sales letters would have trouble selling water in a desert – if they had to rely on the written word. Selling by letter is very different from selling face-to-face, something which must be borne in mind when writing a sales letter.

As with all marketing material, you must engage the reader right from the start. The mistake many writers make is to lead in too gradually. They begin with the background information, progress through the letter to cover the detail, then end with the offer. This is a clear and logical way to write – if you are sure your reader will sit down and read through your letter start to finish. But they won't. That's why you have to turn logic on its head. Hook the reader first. Let them know upfront that you can help them save money, be sexier, attain eternal youth, climb the career ladder ... or whatever. Then go on to explain how.

Like fishing, there are various hooks you can use to catch your reader. They are:

> • *The 'sit up and take notice' statement* – 'You can double your office efficiency overnight'
> • *The amazing fact* – '90 per cent of businesses could get by with just half as many staff. Could yours?'

- *The question you can't ignore* – 'Want to cut your heating bills?' or 'How would you cope if you lost your job tomorrow?'
- *The real-life story* – 'Jeff didn't insure his home. Now he wishes he had. One evening he got home from work and ...'
- *The direct comparison* – 'Jenny James is about the same age as you, but she looks years younger. How? Because she uses ...'
- *The fantastic offer* – 'We're the best bank in town – or your money back'
- *The incentive* – 'You could win a fabulous family holiday in Florida'
- *The trip down 'Memory Lane'* – 'The King's Road was buzzing, flower power was the rage, ethnic fashions were in, and life had never been better. Our 'Hits of the '60s' CDs really capture the mood of the decade ...'
- *The endorsement* – 'The Viking, The Grant Arms, The Green Man, The King's Head – which is the odd one out? You are. They already use Freeman's frozen meals to help them provide the best bar meals in town ...'
- *The testimonial* – ' "Since attending Jack French's public speaking seminar, my confidence has grown 500 per cent. I would have no qualms whatsoever in standing up and talking to 1000 people." What could a Jack French seminar do for your confidence?'
- *Strength in numbers* – 'Two million Scots shop at QuickMark. Do you?'
- *Reappraisal* – 'Think you can't afford a conservatory like this? Think again!'
- *Test results* – 'Recent surveys by independent motoring organizations revealed that our car servicing is the most comprehensive and affordable in ...'

These openers are irresistible. They make you want to know more. Having hooked the reader, lead on with your offer or proposition. How you present this is vital. It's no good writing to people offering a top of the range computer scanner at a good price. That will only sell to those who already want a scanner, know what else is available, and how much they cost. They will know straight off that your 300dpi colour scanner is a bargain at only £150. To everyone else it's meaningless. So how do you present your offer? Well, start by reminding yourself that no one buys products or services *per se*: instead we buy solutions to problems. So if you want to write a sales letter that sells, address that problem upfront – and offer the solution. That way you will be communicating in a meaningful and relevant way with your readers. Let's look at an example. Take the computer scanner:

> ✗ The new MicroCom scanner is a 300dpi scanner complete with OCR software – all for the amazing price of just £150!

This is promoting the product features (in a jargon-laden way), not the benefits. Concentrate on a plain English account of what the product can do for the reader and your copy will be more persuasive. For example:

> ✔ Want to save time on retyping? With our MicroCom scanner, you can scan text in seconds, at the touch of a button, and save on hours of retyping. What's more, it scans photos and illustrations, enabling you to produce top-quality publicity materials straight from your computer. And all for £150! Why pay for an expensive temp or a designer when you can handle picture scanning and retyping in-house at a fraction of the cost and hassle?

The second example is better because it sells a solution to a problem that the reader might have been unaware of until reading the mailing. It therefore sells scanners to those who were never even thinking about getting one. Lead with the solution, then go on to address any objections and questions.

Think carefully about how you word the deal you are offering. You need to make it irresistible. Don't just state the price, emphasize the value. Don't write:

> ✗ Five reams of quality recycled A4 paper for just £15 from Poppington's Paper

write:

> ✔ Poppington's Paper cuts out the middleman. Five reams of quality recycled A4 paper delivered direct to your office for just £15. Why pay more!

If it is a good deal, make it sound that way. Spell it out. Don't assume the reader will know it's a great offer. The words you choose really can have an effect on the bottom line: your company's success. Take the book club offering 'two books for the price of one'. They discovered that the same offer, but worded differently ('buy one, get one free'), was far more effective. Other research has shown that 'buy one, get one free' is more powerful than '50 per cent off'. So remember, you need to have a good offer and to word the offer so it holds maximum attraction.

Other points to bear in mind with sales letters are:

- If you can, offer a 'get-out clause' to reassure readers that you are genuine and bona fide. This can be as simple as: 'Return your books to us within 10 days if you are not completely satisfied and we will give you a full, no-quibble refund'.
- Any guarantees you offer should be highlighted.
- Say clearly what the reader needs to do in order to take up your offer, e.g. 'visit our showroom before the end of June' or 'return the tear-off slip within the next seven days'.
- Set a deadline to create a sense of urgency and prompt an immediate response. 'Hurry. Offer ends on January 31st' is better than 'Take advantage of this special offer now'.
- Make it easy for readers to respond, for example by enclosing a return envelope with a stamp, including your telephone number, or printing an easy-to-complete coupon. (Further ideas on making it easy to respond can be found later in this chapter.)

When writing your covering letter, cover the five Ps. Keep it

- *Punchy:* preferably one side. If you go onto two sides, end page one with a split sentence to encourage the reader to turn the page. (It's OK for enclosures to be lengthy, if appropriate – such as a catalogue – but keep your letter to the point.)
- *Personal:* write in the first person. Be natural and use everyday words. Use a style appropriate for the audience and the subject matter.
- *Persuasive:* put forward powerful reasons why they should buy the product.
- *Pulling:* make sure everything about the package has pulling power, attracting the reader and keeping them.
- *Pushing:* gently push the reader in the right direction, so that they place an order or return a coupon for more information.

Ensure your letter has:

- *A beginning* – the hook
- *A middle* – the facts/detail/proposition (briefly!)
- *An end* – what action is required/a response device

- *A postscript* – this is optional. A hand-written style PS stands out from the rest of the text and can be used to reinforce the offer or encourage action – 'Hurry – offer only available until ...' or 'Remember, we cannot repeat this offer at these spectacular prices, so order today ...'

## Lead-generating letters

A sales letter should generate sales as a result of the letter, whereas a lead-generating letter aims to create a list of strong leads. It weeds out those who are not serious buyers, leaving you with genuine prospects to woo. Lead-generating letters are the first step in the sales process, requiring follow-up in the form of other letters, further information, samples, a telephone call, or some other method.

When you write a letter, be clear whether you are writing a sales letter or a lead-generating one. Lead-generating letters should be fairly short. Don't go into too much detail at this stage: all you are doing is asking someone to show an interest, you are not trying to sell just yet. Many of the rules relating to sales letters also apply to the lead-generating variety.

## Information letters

These letters must flag up at the start what their purpose is. For example:

IMPORTANT SAFETY NOTICE: McSWEENEY PUSH-CHAIRS

MOBILE PHONE: IMPORTANT CHANGE TO BILLING ARRANGEMENTS

JACOB'S SALE STARTS FRIDAY

Then go on to give the detailed information. Spell out what action is required, e.g.

Return your pushchair to any McSweeney's store, where we will fit new safety nuts free of charge.

> Complete the enclosed direct debit form and return it to your bank by 1st September so that the new billing arrangements can be put in place.

## Navigational letters

Navigational letters should be short and clear, with lots of bullet points. For example:

> Thanks for your enquiry about Duson Paints. We enclose:
> - a colour card showing our range of 200+ paints
> - a decorating tips leaflet
> - a brochure containing creative yet easy-to-achieve ideas for using colour in your home
> - a money-off voucher
> - a list of local stockists
>
> If you would like to know anything more about Duson Paints ...

Their aim is to hold a mailing together, to explain what is in it, and to signpost readers to the enclosure(s).

Remember what I said at the beginning of this chapter about the three steps readers need to take?

1 They must open the envelope
2 They must read the contents
3 They must place an order (or take some other desired action)

Follow the advice given so far and you will at least get them through the first two steps. But your ultimate success depends on the ease with which you enable people to respond to your mailing. Use a combination from the list below to ensure that action is easy:

- *Response mechanism:* include an order form, a simple tear-off slip, a coupon or card to allow easy response.
- *Business reply:* paying the postage for your customer's reply increases response. Envelopes or cards pre-printed with your address make it really easy for recipients to respond.
- *Freepost:* your enquirers/respondents can write to you post-free, though you will have to pick up the tab.
- *Freephone:* both British Telecom and Mercury offer Freephone numbers, which work in a similar way to Freepost. Or you can offer a 'lo-call' number, allowing callers to ring you long distance at local telephone rates. Research shows

that people generally prefer to respond by post rather than by telephone.
- *Credit card payment:* if people are able to pay by credit card, it is even easier for them to respond. A Freephone credit card hotline makes it easier still.

Encourage responses by including a 'speed incentive'. For example:

Reply by June 30th and we'll knock 10 per cent off your bill

## Targeting

Think back to Chapter 2 where we looked at audiences. Wherever possible it is best to write for a tight audience. The clearer the audience, the better targeted the messages. The beauty of letters is that they can be tailored to the audience. Unlike an expensive brochure, a letter can be produced in half a dozen completely different versions for little or no extra cost. It means that you can send out the same mailshot, but with a different covering letter, to:

- Existing customers
- Cold prospects
- Warm prospects

making direct mail infinitely flexible.

## Reply cards

Many direct mail packages include a reply card, providing the recipient with an easy way to seek further information. Reply cards can too easily be left until last, and written hurriedly with little thought. After all, they're just a way of capturing interested readers' details, aren't they? No, they are more than that. The reply card is a valuable opportunity to:

- Restate your offer
- Reinforce your message

If you use it simply to build up a mailing list of warm prospects, you are missing a trick. The reply card needs to be copywritten because it is an important selling opportunity. It should look something like this:

> Please send me your FREE information guide to installing a new bathroom, full of great tips and stylish ideas. I understand that I am under NO OBLIGATION to buy, but if I place an order in the next two months I will qualify for a 10 per cent discount.

The reply card allows you to restate your case briefly and powerfully. Don't use it just to collect names and addresses, really get it working for you.

## Testing your words

Direct mail offers the perfect way to test your copy: test mailings. You can systematically change various elements of your copy, and monitor the responses to the mailings to test the effectiveness of different approaches. You could use it to discover what sort of headline, envelope or body copy produced the best results. Do you get a better response with short or longer copy? A test mailing could help you find out. Does an envelope with a printed message make a difference to the quantity and quality of responses? Again, use a test mailing to help you discover. When doing a test mailing, do not introduce more than one variable in each test. Otherwise you will not know which factor led to increased or decreased response. Remember, though, that you can run several test mailings simultaneously.

*Test matrices*

You can split your mailing to try out different things at the same time. For example, let's say you wanted to:

- Try a new mailing list (List X) and to test its performance against the mailing list you usually use (List Y)
- Test your usual plain white envelope against an envelope printed with the message: 'Open now for five ways to save on car maintenance'
- Test the above and the plain envelope, against an envelope printed: 'Valuable savings for motorists'

Your test matrix would look like this:

|  | List Y (usual mailing list) | List X (new list) |
|---|---|---|
| Usual pack with plain envelope (control) | A | B |
| 'Five ways to save ...' envelope | A1 |  |
| 'Valuable savings ...' envelope | A2 |  |

To find out whether your new list was better than your existing list, you would need to compare the results of A with B. This is done using a control, namely, your standard mailing pack. However, you also want to find out whether other factors affect response. Comparing the results of A, A1 and A2 will tell you what sort of envelope works best.

You can carry on testing until you find the most successful combination of factors. To know which mailings are more successful, you need to code the response device. You can do this by writing or printing a code (e.g. M1, M2 or M3) on the coupon or form that the respondent returns to you.

# 13 Advertising

This chapter explains how we read adverts and shows how to write them, whether for the press or radio. It takes a close look at the various components of an ad, such as the headline and the body text, and tells how to put together an effective advert. There's advice on how to stay within the law by following the advertising codes.

Advertising executives are perhaps the most envied of marketing professionals. They get to deal with big budgets and prestigious assignments, to work with the stars and parade their work for the world to admire. True? Well, most people who work in advertising would not recognize this description. Advertising is generally a lot less glamorous than we think, yet the aura and the mystique surrounding advertising tend to put off would-be copywriters from trying to write advertising copy themselves. Don't let it deter you. You can write advertising copy, even if you never reach the heights of Saatchi & Saatchi.

For advertising, as with any copywriting assignment, before you even put pen to paper you must do your homework.

- *Understand your audience* – to communicate effectively you need to know who you are writing for.
- *Know the competition* – if you know what they are offering, you can offer something better, or differentiate yourself in some other way.
- *Know your UBP* – your Unique Buying Point. This is different from a USP (Unique Selling Point – see page 15); it focuses on what counts for the buyer. USPs are product-centred.
- *Know your benefits* – you will know from Chapter 2 that you should sell benefits, not features (see page 14).

Once you have done the groundwork, it is time to start on your advert. Lesson 1: good advertising should employ the AIDA formula. AIDA is an acronym standing for Attention, Interest, Desire and Action.

- Your advert will be competing with many others, so it must stand out and attract *Attention* if you want it noticed (a vital precursor to its being read).

- It must engage the reader's *Interest* so that they will keep reading (or listening or watching). If you cannot maintain interest, you will lose your readers long before you have convinced them to buy.
- It should stimulate *Desire* – to buy your products or use your service.
- It must prompt *Action* – what use is an arresting advert that encourages interest and desire, if no action results? Your advert must make it easy for readers/listeners to take the necessary action.

## Attention

For print ads (radio adverts are looked at later in this chapter), strong photographs, bold design, bright colours (or striking use of black and white in a colour publication), or a combination of these can help achieve something that gets noticed. Of course, it's down to your designer to come up with these. From the copy side, arresting headlines can be great attention-grabbers. You can read how to write a powerful headline later in this chapter.

Another technique for attracting attention is to make topical references in your ads. Here are two examples which illustrate what I am talking about.

During a national postal strike, Internet provider Pipex placed the following press advert:

> TODAY IT'S E-MAIL OR NO MAIL ... We'd like to thank today's striking postal workers for the opportunity to bring the cause of e-mail to the notice of the British public. There's not much to say about e-mail except that it's faster, cheaper and more flexible than ordinary mail ... Oh, and it never goes on strike.

In the run-up to National Tyre Safety Week Kwik-Fit ran this ad:

> SOMEONE WILL PROBABLY CHECK YOUR TYRES NEXT WEEK. MAKE SURE IT'S OUR BOYS IN BLUE.
> Next week ... police will be stopping cars to check the condition of their tyres. If you are found to have tyres that are ... you could be fined up to £2500 and 3 penalty points for EACH tyre. Call Kwik-Fit first. We'll give you a free report ...

The topical link makes the adverts more relevant and, therefore, more likely to be read.

## Interest

Having got the reader's interest, you must retain it. Use over-long copy, complicated messages, or pompous/obscure language and you will lose your readers. To keep readers, keep copy lively and your message simple yet interesting.

## Desire

This is where creativity enters the frame. You need to find a way to create desire for your goods or service. How deep a desire depends on the product. If you are selling expensive cars, you need to create craving, envy, longing. You therefore select words or conjure up images to nurture that desire (luxury, speed, status). But if you are selling lavatory cleaner, the desire is somewhat different. It might be based on need (the need to have a clean and hygienic WC in order to avoid smells, infection, etc.) or practicality (ease of use, etc.). But either way, no desire, no sale.

## Action

Action is the acid test of an advert's effectiveness. Many award-winning ads are high on style, low on action. However great your advert looks, or however beautifully it reads, it is worthless if it fails, as the expression goes, 'to get bums on seats'. Your advert must make clear what action is required, prompt readers to take it, and enable them to do so with ease. There are various ways to make action easy, which we looked at in more detail in the previous chapter:

- Coupons
- Freepost address
- Freephone number
- Simple return address: always use one that is as short as possible and easy to spell.

Before you decide which action-easing device(s) to offer, first be clear on what action you want readers to take. Do you want them to:

- Visit your store?
- Place an order?
- Ask you for a quotation for work?
- Complete a coupon requesting more information or a free publicity pack?

- Send for a free sample?
- Call you for details of a product or service?
- Take out membership?
- Change their buying behaviour (e.g. by switching to your product)?

Look at your completed advert and ask yourself: 'Is it clear what the reader has to do? Have I made it easy for them?' Pay attention to what you are asking your reader to do, and ensure you are specific about what action is required. Never use a vague expression like:

> ✗ We hope to hear from you soon

Be specific and directive:

> ✔ Return this coupon today

or:

> ✔ Contact us before July 1st to take advantage of this great offer

## How we 'read' adverts

Successful ads follow the AIDA formula, but it takes more than a simple formula to make a great ad. You also need to understand how adverts work. That involves knowing how they are read. Research in this area has shown that there is a definite route, or 'eyepath' which we follow on first seeing an advert.

1  *Picture* – we look at this first.
2  *Headline* – then we move to the headline. 80 per cent of readers stop there.
3  *Bottom right-hand corner* – those still reading move here next, which is where most advertisers place their name and logo. Few will go further than this.
4  *Caption* – for those who do, the caption on the photo or illustration is the bit they read next.
5  *Cross-heading* – this is followed by a scan of the cross-headings, subheadings, other illustrations and graphs, and so on.
6  *Body text* – only then do people begin on the 'body text' – the main part of your advert.

So if you put all your effort into the body text, you'll be ignoring the massive 80 per cent plus of readers who never get this far! The lesson is simple: do not rely on body text. If your picture and headline fail to attract, you might as well not bother with body copy.

*Pictures plus headlines*

Since your picture and headline are the first ports of call for your readers, these are the parts of your advert that must be given special attention. They must work together, with each telling its half of the story. The headline must not simply say what the picture shows, it needs to work harder than that. Each needs the other to make sense. Together they should produce a powerful message stronger than the sum of the individual parts.

Of course, not every advert needs a photograph or illustration, but each should have a headline. Should you decide to use a picture, choosing the right one is the job of your designer, but writing a great headline is your department. Only one in five will read beyond it, so use it well.

*Headlines*

The function of the headline is:

- To create an immediate impact
- To attract attention
- To attract the right prospects
- To lure readers into reading your body text

Like many things, headlines can be classified. There are various types of headline, the main ones being:

- Direct
- Indirect
- 'How to'
- Questions
- Commands

*Direct headlines*

These headlines get straight to the point. For example:

Cheddar. Only £1 a 1lb at Sainsway

or:

> OVER 500 USED CARS AT EVERY PITSTOP SHOWROOM
> – GUARANTEED

The strength of these headlines is they get a complete message across. The drawback is that they are so complete as to make it unnecessary for the reader to delve into the body text. But you can write direct headlines that get a point across, while also leading the reader into the copy. Look at the two examples above, then see below how a little rewriting can lead readers from headline to text.

> **How Sainsway can sell cheddar at only £1 a 1lb**
> Our competitors will charge you twice this. Because we cut back on the fripperies – fancy in-store displays, expensive promotion and packaging – we can offer you top quality products at bargain basement prices. Lower overheads mean lower prices. So you gain.

> **How can Pitstop Showrooms guarantee you a choice of over 500 used cars?**
> Easy. As the top name dealer in used cars we have the resources to carry a huge stock. That means more choice for you, and better value too.

Now you have direct headlines that are strong in their own right, with the benefit that they also encourage the reader to find out more. Direct headlines can also be used to attract the right prospects:

> CALLING ALL MUMS AND DADS
> Cheap ways to keep your kids occupied this summer

or:

> CHOCOHOLICS!
> If you like chocolate, you'll love our new gourmet chocolate shop

or:

> Paying too much for your petrol?

In the first two examples the intended audiences are, literally, spelt out: mums, dads and chocoholics. In the third one, the audience (car owners) is alerted in a less forthright way.

In all these examples, the headlines require the body text to explain them. If you have body text, your headline should encourage readers to read it. But, of course, there is no reason why you must use body text. An advert that is nothing more than a headline, such as:

> London to Manchester only £20 return by rail

is fine. The direct headline, as a stand-alone, can have great impact.

### Indirect headlines

Indirect headlines attract interest and curiosity, but require the right body copy if they are to make any sense at all. For example:

> PURE HEAVEN

This headline might attract your attention, but what does it mean? You need to read the rest of the advert to find out:

> PURE HEAVEN
> ZZ-Beds are so comfortable that we *guarantee* you the deepest, longest and purest sleep you have ever had. It's the closest you will get to heaven on earth.

### 'How to' headlines

These headlines are what they sound:

> How to choose a new vacuum cleaner

> How to get free radiators

You need not spell out the 'how to' bit. You can just imply it:

> Crisp chips – without a deep fat fryer

Effectively this headline is saying: 'How to get crisp chips without a deep fat fryer'.

*Question headlines*

With question headlines the question must be phrased in such a way as to demand an answer:

> Do you want your next car to cost you less?

Sometimes you can ask a question without asking a question:

> Why mothers prefer Poopers Nappies

Strictly speaking this is not a question, but effectively it is. It is asking: 'Would you like to know why mothers prefer Poopers Nappies?' By adding 'why' you make your readers curious. 'Mothers prefer Poopers Nappies' is more likely to leave readers thinking 'so what?'.

*Command headlines*

These headlines (politely) instruct the reader:

> Cut out this coupon. Cut out the middleman

> Be careful. Fireworks can kill

It has been shown that headlines that offer the promise of a reward attract more attention. The reward need not be of the 'buy one get one free' type, where you are offering a genuine financial reward. It can be a promise: 'Sleep easy tonight', for example.

*Subheadings*

Sometimes the main headline has a subordinate headline immediately below it. For example:

> [photo of a top of the range hi-fi]
> **IMAGINE OWNING THIS**
> You could, for just £10 a month

Subheads can help you expand on the point of the main headline, adding more information or detail – but not so much that the subhead becomes body text.

*Headline length*

Like the proverbial piece of string, no one can tell you exactly how long a headline should be. There is no optimum length: a headline should be as long as it needs to be to get the message across. If it can be done in one word, fine. If it takes twenty, fine, so long as it is neither longer nor shorter than it should be, fine.

## The body text

Although 80 per cent of those looking at your advert will not get this far, that's no excuse to pay your body text less attention. Anyone reading it is likely to be interested in what you have to say.

Your body text should:

- Explain your headline
- Explain your photo/illustration, if you used one
- Give more detail
- Present any relevant and compelling facts and information
- Draw the reader in and keep them hooked

It should not:

- Waffle
- Try to say too much
- Use the third person
- Present too many ideas or propositions
- Use too much unbroken text or small print

Like headlines, there are different types of body text:

*Reason-why:* this is where you make a statement and then go on to explain or justify it, offering reasons that appeal to logic. Essentially you are telling your reader why they should buy your product. For example:

THE BEST PEAS IN THE WORLD
That's quite a claim, we know, but who else can match our standards? Delicious organically grown peas, specially selected for flavour and bite. Each pea is inspected for quality and freshness, and we think nothing of rejecting up to 60% ...

*Descriptive:* this kind of copy can be a little dull. It simply describes a product or service.

*Humour:* this kind of copy can be great – but you need to be truly funny for it to work. Humorous copy can be the most difficult for a novice to write effectively.

*Testimonial:* this is where someone testifies to a product's quality, value or features. For example:

> Suzi Hampton has lost count of the number of awards won by her restaurant, Zucchi's. Les Routiers. Egon Ronay. You name it, she's won it. It's her appreciation of fine food, and her absolute refusal to accept anything but the best, that has brought Zucchi's the world acclaim it deserves.
>
> At home, too, Suzi will not compromise on quality. That's why she insists on Chan's rice ...

### Body text length

Short copy is better than long copy, but only if it contains all the information readers want. There's no point in keeping it short for the sake of it, if that means leaving out a mass of information that is required by the reader before they will be willing to take any action. Keep it as short or as long as it needs to be.

### Captions

If you are using photos, graphs and other illustrations, failure to caption them is a missed opportunity. Captions attract twice the readership of your body text, so they are a key way of getting your message across. But do be creative. Never simply state what is in the picture, add to it. So if you have a photo of John Jackson, coffee importer, don't caption the photo:

> ✗ John Jackson, coffee importer

caption it:

> ✔ As a coffee importer, John Jackson knows a thing or two about coffee. And the coffee he chooses to drink is ...

## Style and meaning

In the early days of advertising, long before today's sophisticated techniques and analysis, advertising used to focus on the virtues of a product. Some advertising still does, but increasingly we see advertising creating unique style and meaning for products that are otherwise identical or very similar. Car adverts, for example, don't always focus on practical considerations like fuel consumption, road safety, or speed. (Having said that, Daewoo uses this approach to differentiate it from other car manufacturers.) So many car ads sell a lifestyle or a fantasy. Sociologists and cultural analysts see these style ads as a genre. Often, adverts use other adverts as their reference points.

You need to decide what kind of advert you want:

- Creative (selling a style/image) or
- Informative (selling the benefits of a product)

Your copy for the same product will be very different, depending on which you opt for. You should be able to tell which is which from the following fictitious car adverts.

> Dinner at Maxim's then on to Nicole's film premiere. After that it was party, party, party. If only we had the staying power of the Roverette!

> 50 mpg in heavy traffic. 0–60 on the open road. Room for two adults, three squealing children, one muddy dog and loadsa suitcases and toys. That's the Roverette.

Although the first advert seems to be selling a car, really it's selling a dream. The reader doesn't really believe that they will have such a glamorous and cosmopolitan lifestyle simply by buying a Roverette, but the image nevertheless rubs off. In the second advert the emphasis is on the car's features, which are presented in a very down-to-earth style. So the same car can have quite different images, depending on where you position it through your copy.

## Scepticism

We're no fools, the good old British public. We know how advertising can manipulate us and often we approach adverts with scepticism. We need to be convinced. Some adverts play on our scepticism, like this one for Guinness:

> 'Advertising is legalized lying'
> HG Wells

That's all the ad says! Presumably we are meant to share the joke with them, or to believe that an advertiser so honest about the unprincipled world of advertising must be trusted. Or perhaps it is more subtle than all this. I'd be interested to hear from the person who devised the ad. But seriously, do remember that people reading your advert will do so with a certain amount of suspicion and mistrust.

## Dominance of design

There was a time when the copywriter was king. Think back to old editions of *The Times*, where adverts were entirely text-based. Take a look at the ads in *The Times* today and you will see how dramatically advertising has changed. Increasingly the role of copywriter is being undermined by the emphasis on design in advertising. Images are frequently more important in advertising than text. Indeed, some ads feature no text at all, such as those for Silk Cut cigarettes (aside from the government warning that the product may kill you!). As a copywriter you need to be aware of trends in advertising and not to feel threatened by them. Even if an ad is to feature just a couple of words, dwarfed by a huge illustration, there is still enormous skill for the copywriter in selecting those two very important words.

## Classifieds

Classified adverts require a completely different style to display ads. (Classifieds are small adverts comprising lines of text and no design element. They are grouped by subject, e.g. Restaurants, Talks, Pets, Plumbers. Generally you are charged by the line, so words are at a premium. The more words, the higher the cost.) As a copywriter of classified ads you must:

- Abbreviate ('des res', not 'desirable residence'. 'b&w' for 'black and white' etc.)
- Miss out words (don't bother with words like 'a', 'the', 'is' etc.)
- Forget complete sentences

Don't write:

> There will be a talk on the carpets of Persia, to be held in Softon's rug department. It will take place on Monday, July 10th at 5.30 pm. Tea, coffee and light refreshments will be served. Anyone may attend. [38 words]

Write:

> **Persian Rugs Talk.** Softon's. July 10th. 5.30 pm. Refreshments. All welcome. [10 words]

Although only a quarter as long, the second is as effective as the first – and costs less in column centimetres.

As well as lineage adverts (like the one above) you can have display classifieds. A mistake many companies and organizations make with these is to lead with the company name. For example:

> ## CITY DOG HOME
> 30 Castle Street
> Jacksonville
> (01441) 433521
> Help us help dogs in distress. Make a donation today.

> ## JO JO'S BISTRO
> 37 High Street
> Jacksonville
> (01441) 344351
> Scrummy Cajun cooking and affordable prices.

Small adverts like this still have to follow the same rules as big adverts. A simple rejigging can achieve this. See how much more effective the above two ads are now:

> ## HELP US HELP DOGS IN DISTRESS
> City Dog Home
> 30 Castle Street
> Jacksonville
> (01441) 433521
> Make a donation today.

---

**Scrummy Cajun cooking and affordable prices**
Jo Jo's Bistro
37 High Street
Jacksonville
(01441) 344351

---

The copy is identical but the order has been changed, ensuring that the adverts attract that all-important attention through a powerful headline.

## Keeping within the law

All advertising must be legal, decent, honest and truthful. The Advertising Standards Authority investigates complaints about advertisements and ensures that advertising meets the standard and is in the public interest. The Committee of Advertising Practice (CAP) devises and enforces the British Codes of Advertising and Sales Promotion. They produce a guide to the codes, which is available free of charge. CAP also offer a free and confidential advice service to advertisers, to help ensure that they stay within the Codes. (Ring 0171 580 4100 for details.)

The Codes apply to adverts in newspapers, magazines, catalogues, mailings, brochures and posters, but not to broadcast commercials on TV and radio. These are policed by the Independent Television Commission and the Radio Authority respectively. A full copy of the Codes is available: get hold of one if you are planning any advertising. The main points are:

1　All adverts should be legal, decent, honest and truthful.
2　All adverts should be prepared with a sense of responsibility to consumers and society.
3　Advertisers must hold documentary evidence to prove all claims which are capable of objective substantiation.
4　If there is a significant division of informed opinion about any claims made, they should not be portrayed as universally agreed.
5　No advert should cause fear or distress without good reason. Advertisers should not use shocking claims or images merely to attract attention.

Now to other forms of advertising. It has been suggested that we see between 1000 and 1500 sales messages every day, on TV, buses, posters and so on. Of these we remember only about seven: the other 1493 just pass us by! It is not easy to get your ads into the memorable category, but it should be your aim.

## Bus adverts

There are two types of bus adverts: internals and externals. External advertising must be short and simple. You are advertising on a moving vehicle to people who are themselves on the move. If you have too much copy, it will be impossible to read. A short statement or headline, combined (possibly) with a grabbing graphic, is sufficient. So forget cramming in everything about your product or service. Develop a clear and simple message and stick with it.

Internal advertising, on the other hand, can be more expansive; it will be read by people with time to kill – people sitting on buses. You can go into a bit more detail, but remember that you are limited by space, and your text must be large enough to be seen across the bus.

## Radio adverts

Radio adverts are a fantastic vehicle for creative writers. Unlike TV, on radio you can do almost anything, like visiting far-off or remote places; or doing impossible things (such as going back in time). Because you are relying on sound effects, not special (and expensive) visual effects, you can do so much more. But radio ads do have their drawbacks:

- You cannot show the product
- You cannot show phone numbers, addresses, the 'small print'

This does create problems for the copywriter, but they are not insurmountable.

Your initial challenge with a radio advert, as with a print ad, is to attract attention. You need to stand out from the other ads in the commercial break. That means sounding different to them. You can sound different through the copy, the way the copy is read, and any sound effects used. But remember that radio is not a visual medium, unlike press and TV ads. (I know it's obvious, but many home-grown radio ads seem to ignore that fact!) So write to be heard, not seen.

The average commercial is 30 seconds, which gives you around 70 words. It's not a lot, especially as you are relying on sound, with no pictures to back you up. But you can use sound to the full, letting it enhance your script. The most memorable type of radio advertising is 'mood/fantasy'. This type of advertising does not shout at the listener, it involves them, painting a picture in their mind.

Ensure your ad talks directly to your listener, and in the same way that they would speak. To write in this way you need to have in your mind a picture of the average listener. The radio station will be able to supply you with a very accurate profile of their listeners (which may vary according to the time of day). Think about this typical listener, their likes and dislikes – even about where they will be listening to your ad. (Seventy-two per cent of listeners listen to their radios in the kitchen, but 43 per cent of 15- to 24-year-olds listen in the bathroom. Ask the radio station for their local statistics.)

Most listeners will not be in the market for your product at the time of the ad – but you want them to listen all the same. If your ad makes the necessary impact, they will think about you next time they want to buy one of your products. To achieve this your ads should be interesting, engaging, entertaining or funny – or all four.

Like other advertising, radio requires a clear signal to the listener of what action they must take. You need to tell them:

- Where they can buy your product, or
- Which number to ring for further information (preferably a Freephone number, and something easy to recall), and/or
- Where to write to for details – addresses must be short and easy

# 14 News releases

There's more to writing an effective news release than most marketers and business people realize. This chapter explains the five Ws of release-writing, how to find a news angle, and how to write a release that stands a chance of getting into print.

When you look at your local or national newspaper, a fair amount of what you read will be derived from a news release (sometimes known as a 'press release', though best referred to as a news release if you wish to avoid upsetting the broadcast media). Marketing people eager to promote their products and their company for free in the media need to be able to write good releases that stand a reasonable chance of hitting the headlines.

If you write a good news release based on a sound storyline, there is a high chance that a newspaper (radio or TV station) will use it. But if you don't know what you are doing, your news release will end up in the bin, with the scores (in some cases, hundreds) of others that didn't make the grade that day. So what exactly is a news release and how do you write a good one?

*What is a release?*

A release is a summary of information about your company, work or products, written in the style of a news report and typed double spaced. It is organized and laid out in a certain way. Here's an example:

---

For immediate use
Tuesday, 28 October 1997

**JOBS BOOST FOR WEST MIDLANDS**
**250 NEW JOBS IN BAKING INDUSTRY**

Sitwell's Bakery has announced that it is to create 250 new jobs in the West Midlands by the end of the year.

The opening of four new shops in the Birmingham area will create 100 new jobs and a further 150 jobs will be provided at the company's main bakery in Wolverhampton. Around 100 of these will be baking apprenticeships for young people, with the remaining 50 being clerical jobs.

Said Maria Maitkin, Chief Executive of Sitwell's: 'At a time when other companies are laying off staff, we are delighted to have good news for unemployed people in the West Midlands. We are offering quality jobs with training and real prospects. This represents a real boost to the local economy and real hope to local people who are currently jobless.'

The expansion at Sitwell's has been brought about following a cash injection from investors, who recently took up a share offer which has enabled the company to invest in the latest computer-controlled baking equipment.

If the West Midlands expansion is a success, as the company predicts, further initiatives will be launched in the north of England and in Scotland, creating up to 750 further new jobs.

ends

**For further information contact:**
Maria Maitkin, Chief Executive 01902 212127 (office) 0121 444
276 1232 (home)
or David Caruthers, Head of Personnel 01902 212127 (office)
01902 458650 (home)

A release's advantage over advertising is that it can help you secure some powerful, persuasive and free media coverage. Because your copy appears as editorial, it tends to be perceived by readers as more credible and independent than a piece of advertising. The obvious drawback is that there are no guarantees. With advertising, your copy appears word for word as you wrote it, it appears on the day you want it, and in the press you want it in. When you write a news release, there is no guarantee that it will appear at all, let alone that it will be reproduced in the form you would wish. It might be edited or completely rewritten. Unlike most other pieces of marketing material, it is written in the third person.

*What makes a good release?*

- One that promotes your service, product or message and is, at the same time, a 'good read'
- One that avoids 'PR puffery' – releases overselling a product and using exaggerated claims and hyperbole do not get published
- One that is newsworthy
- One that is not blatantly commercial

As the media always receive more releases than they can use, you need to ensure that yours is the one that leaps out from the pile, instantly grabbing the news editor's attention and interest.

## Ingredients of a successful release

- A gripping first paragraph
- A strong news angle
- The 'five Ws' – who, what, when, where and why
- A quote from a named person
- If appropriate, a 'Note to Editors'
- A contact name
- A home phone number
- A date

## A gripping first paragraph

Like any marketing material that you write, the first paragraph of your news release is all-important. If you get the first paragraph of a direct mail letter wrong, you can't expect the recipient to read on to the second paragraph. So too with the news release. A busy news editor will glance at your release, but will read no further unless you have hooked them.

Many releases make a common mistake: they progress logically through a story, starting with the background and building up to the news. The opposite is required. You need to lead with the news, then explain the background.

## A strong news angle

All releases must be interesting and have some genuine news value. Finding an interesting news angle can be difficult. Suppose you want some publicity for the launch of a new perfume. At your company the new perfume might be big news. You have worked on its formulation for years and the company's future relies on a successful consumer launch. But what is immensely important to companies is generally not in the least bit interesting to those outside them. Somehow you have to spice up your news to make it relevant and to add newsiness. If you wrote:

> ✗ Harmony, makers of some of the world's favourite perfume, today launch a new fragrance – Imagination.

you would find that you attracted zero coverage (except, possibly, in the perfume trade press). How could you add the necessary fizz? You could try creating some kind of event to add news value:

> ✔ Three of the world's most beautiful women jetted into London today to become the first to wear Imagination, an exclusive perfume that ounce for ounce costs more than pure gold.

This sort of story would get good picture coverage and would have appeal for tabloid newspapers. Or you could focus on some aspect of the product that is newsy, such as:

> ✔ The controversial *avant-garde* artist Damien Hirst's latest creation is guaranteed to create a stir – for being too traditional! Famous for his pickled animal carcasses, the artist's newest work is likely to be sitting on the dressing tables of respectable ladies across the country by the end of the year, for he has designed the scent bottle for a new perfume, Imagination, which goes on sale today.

Which approach you take must depend on how you want to position your product.

To help you find your newsworthy angle, try asking:

- Is what we are doing the biggest or the best?
- Is it a first?
- Is it special in some way?
- What will it mean for our customers?
- What will it mean for the country/city?
- Is there something different, unusual or even unique about it?
- Are we breaking new ground?
- Are we creating new jobs?
- Will we change the way people live or work?

## The five Ws

Journalists learn early on that every story must cover the 'Five Ws'. These stand for:

**Who** – who is doing it? (e.g. your company, a celebrity)
**What** – what are they doing? (launching a new product, making a major announcement)
**When** – when are they doing it?
**Where** – where are they doing it?
**Why** – why are they doing it? (to satisfy customer demand, to become a market leader)

When you write a release, go back over it and check that you have covered your five Ws. But be careful not to open your release using the five Ws formula, as it will make for a rather dull read – as you can see from the following example:

---

For immediate use
Monday, 3 November 1997

**SALE OF 1960s TOYS**

Acton's Sale Rooms in High Street, Peterton, will be holding an auction of 1960s toys at 2 pm on Saturday 8 November.
Said Jeremy Dulcie-Chives, chief auctioneer at Acton's: 'Acton's is the South West's premier auction house. We are now entering our centenary year, providing an auction service to over 100 000 people each year.'
Items on sale will include dolls, trainsets, toys and boardgames.
Viewing from 10 am to 7 pm all day Friday, 7 November.

**For more information contact:**
Jeremy Dulcie-Chives, Acton's chief auctioneer
Tel. 76528 (sale rooms) or 223667 (home).

---

The version below is far livelier and offers more scope to editors to do an interesting feature:

---

For immediate use
Monday, 3 November 1997

**PRICEY BLONDE BOMBSHELL
TO PULL CROWDS IN PETERTON**

A desirable blonde bombshell in her 30s will be star attraction at next week's auction at Acton's Sale Rooms in Peterton. The early Barbie doll is just one of the lots at the sale of 1960s collectable toys taking place in the town on Saturday (8 November).
Said Jeremy Dulcie-Chives, chief auctioneer at Acton's: 'We expect a lot of people to turn out for a good reminisce. They will be able to see toys they have not seen since their childhood, such as Barbie, Cindy and Tressy dolls, Hornby Dublo trainsets, Thunderbirds memorabilia, and classic boardgames which have long since disappeared from the shelves of our toyshops.'
Would-be buyers will, however, need more than Monopoly money to pay for their purchases. The original Barbie doll, for example, is expected to go under the hammer for around £500.

---

> The auction takes place at 2 pm at Acton's Sale Rooms in the High Street. Viewing from 10 am to 7 pm all day Friday, 7 November.
>
> ends
>
> **For more information contact:**
> Jeremy Dulcie-Chives, Acton's chief auctioneer
> Tel. 76528 (sale rooms) or 223667 (home).

This contains the five Ws, but a lot more besides.

## Quote

Every release should feature a quote from a named, relevant person. Newspapers like this, as it makes their readers believe that they actually interviewed you, when really they just used your release! Make your quote interesting and believable. Do not use the quote to peddle hype and nonsense. Do not, for example, write:

> ✗ Joe Smith, Managing Director of Harmony Perfumes, said: 'Imagination is a sophisticated scent for sophisticated women. Anyone with style will be wearing Imagination this season.'

Make your quote newsy and knowledgeable:

> ✔ Joe Smith, Managing Director of Harmony Perfumes, said: 'There is a bewildering choice in the scent market, and our research shows that consumers are looking for differentiation. Our target woman wants a fragrance that says something about her. She is well-educated, interested in the arts, and has spending power. We commissioned Damien Hirst to design our bottle because ...'

This quote adds something to the story; the first one is mere puffery.

Unlike other material that you write, it is possible that your news release will be rewritten by someone else: a reporter. You should therefore write your release with editing in mind. Sometimes newspapers cut a story to fit a space. It is therefore sensible to write your release so that it can be chopped paragraph by paragraph from the bottom up and still make sense.

## Note to editors

Some releases include a 'Note to Editors' at the end. This is where you include background information that is useful or interesting, but not vital to the story. It helps keep your release shorter, but ensures that you don't leave out something that could be useful to the reporter. You might, for example, write:

> **Note to Editors:**
> 1 Harmony makes 27 different fragrances, including Shame, Rebelette and Roses.
> 2 Harmony, voted Perfumier of the Year 1998, has an annual turnover of £330 million.

## A contact name

Every release should contain at least one contact person, and preferably two. If a journalist wants to check anything in your release, they will call one of the named contacts. Your contacts should, therefore, be easy to get hold of, confident about talking to the media, and fully briefed.

## A home phone number

Few journalists work nine to five, so out-of-hours contact numbers are essential. Include mobile phone numbers too.

## A date

If you fail to display a date prominently on your release, it may be assumed to be old news. Demonstrate that your release is bang up to date by showing its current date.

## Targeting

As with direct mail, so with news releases: target. Would you send the same direct mail package to hot prospects as to cold ones? Probably not. Nor should you send the same release to everyone. The needs of local papers are different from those of the trade press. Write in a way that will appeal to the target group of publications. This might mean producing three or four different releases, but it's worth it if it secures more coverage for you. A release to the national press would aim to create a good general read. One to the trade press might focus more on technical matters that would be understood by its specialist readers. Clearly a release to the local press would require a local angle.

## News release musts

1 Releases must be short: preferably one page but no more than two.
2 No release should contain jargon (unless it is for the trade press), hype, clichés, or any unexplained abbreviations.
3 Use clear, positive language and short words and sentences to make your release snappy.
4 Don't get carried away by detail. Concentrate on the essentials and stick to the facts.

A release with the right content stands a good chance of making it into print. But that's just part of the story. You must also ensure that you set out your release properly, according to convention.

## Making it look right

To maximize your chances of getting your release used, make sure that your release looks right.

- Double-space your releases – so they can be easily edited
- Use wide margins – to allow for editing
- Keep releases single-sided
- Use your A4 headed notepaper for the top sheet, but plain white paper for continuation sheets
- Avoid fancy formatting – do not underline, put words in bold, italics, capitals and so on
- Never split a sentence from one page to the next. Ideally, don't let a paragraph continue over the page
- Staple pages together – it's easy for paper-clipped pages to get separated in a busy newsroom

If you get the style and content of your release right, you lay it out properly, and you get your timing right, sit back and look forward to some valuable news coverage.

# 15 Articles and features

Most business people and marketing managers are called upon from time to time (or more often than that) to write articles for a variety of outlets – the trade press, local press, in-house journals and customer newsletters. Find out in this chapter how to produce readable and interesting articles with relative ease.

Although writing an article is not that difficult, many people are put off trying because they fear that it is. Part of their concern is that their work will be published, with their name on it, for all the world to see. If you're a duff writer, everyone will know when they read you in print. Fear not! With a bit of planning and research, you will be able to write readable articles.

If you have to write a piece, you will make the task easier if you make sure you know, right at the outset:

- *Audience* – who you are writing for. An article aimed at mechanical engineers will be rather different from one written for the general public.
- *Publication* – will it appear in a learned journal or an informal staff newsletter?
- This will help you decide on *style* and language. You also need to know:
- *Length* – it is easier to write to a certain length than to have to drastically lengthen or shorten an article afterwards.
- *Deadline* – do you have three weeks or just three hours to produce your copy?
- *Subject* – what are you to write about? Get as detailed a brief as possible. If, for example, your brief is to write about your company, ask further questions. Its history? Its current activities overall? An aspect of its work, such as its research and development department? Its predictions for the future?
- *Purpose* – what is the purpose of your article? Is it to entertain, to educate, to inform?
- *Context* – it helps to know the context in which your article will appear. Will it be one of several articles exploring different aspects of the same subject, for example? If so, you must find out what other articles are being prepared, by whom, and on what areas.

Now you have a clear idea of what is expected of you. Time now to get down to some hard graft. As you read in the first part of this book, there are five stages to producing copy. These stages apply as much to article and feature writing as they do to other copywriting assignments. To recap, they are:

- *Collect* – dump down any thoughts and ideas
- *Group* – organize your ideas into themes
- *Order* – put your themes in order
- *Place* – decide what will go where and how much space each bit should have
- *Write* – start writing and produce an initial draft
- *Revise* – reread and improve your first and subsequent drafts until you are happy with your finished work

Every article should have a theme, argument, 'big idea' or hypothesis to hold it together. Decide on your theme and then write the article around it.

Rather like a news release, an article relies upon its first paragraph to hook the reader. Write a dull opener and your reader might give up on you. To attract interest from the outset it helps to open with one of the following:

- *A controversial statement* – 'Murder, theft and other crimes would be drastically reduced if hard drugs were legalized ...'
- *An amazing fact or statistic* – 'The average housecat walks roughly 10 kilometres every day...'
- *An interesting or moving personal story* – 'David looks like any other boy, only he's not. Unlike his pals at nursery, David will not be around to celebrate his fifth birthday: he is dying of an incurable ...'
- *A cryptic comment* that appears to have no relevance to the story, ensuring that the reader reads on to discover the link

Whatever approach you take, make sure your opener is relevant to your reader. Take the example below of an article I wrote for a daily newspaper:

We hear from time to time in the news about doctors being struck off. It is the ultimate punishment for a doctor who is found guilty of gross misconduct – such as having sex with a patient, killing or harming someone in their care by administering the wrong drug, or committing some other major error or misdemeanour. But we

> never hear about the patients who are struck off. Unlike doctors, patients don't need to commit an offence for it to happen to them. And unlike the doctors, they don't get a hearing and they can't appeal. They don't even have the right to find out why they were struck off.

The focus of the article is on patients, for more patients than doctors read national newspapers. Here's another article I wrote on the same subject, this time written for a specialist publication aimed at GPs:

> Imagine this. It's Monday morning at your surgery. Your receptionist comes in with your coffee and post. Just an ordinary day. A GMC frank catches your eye and you open the envelope. The letter it contains tells you that you have been struck off their register. Surely there must be some mistake? You have done nothing wrong. You have not had a hearing, to your knowledge there have been no complaints about you. You reach for the phone. The GMC tell you that they will not reveal why you have been struck off, they do not want to hear what you have to say, you have no right to an appeal and you must accept the decision. Furthermore, the removal comes into effect in just seven days. How would you feel if that happened to you? Now you know how the tens of thousands of people involuntarily removed from their GPs' lists each year feel. Bewildered. Shocked. Incredulous.

My aim in the second article is to get doctors to put themselves in their patients' shoes. So in each case the article is on the same subject, but the approach taken is tailored to the audience and their experiences. That's why you must find out who you are writing for, so you can ensure a relevant read for them.

In each of the above articles I used case histories to bring the article to life. I described real people, how they came to be struck off, and their feelings about the experience. Case histories are a good technique in feature writing. They can be used to bring a human touch to an article that might otherwise be too abstract or issue-based to elicit the right reader response. Sometimes you can open the story with one person's experience, then open it out to discuss wider issues.

## Coping with short attention spans

As a writer you need to be mindful of your readers' willingness to tackle your piece. In today's sound-bite culture, there is a growing unwillingness among many to read anything that looks lengthy or complex. However much you may abhor this trend, you must recognize it and cater for the needs of today's reader.

You should start by assuming that your article will not be read start to finish: if it is, that's a bonus. Many readers will start by scanning your article, reading on only if something stands out and grabs their attention. That's why you should include interesting subheads, to entrap the scanners.

Next, you have the dippers. These readers will read through the bits that stand out: call-outs, boxes, bullet points, charts and tables, etc. (see page 38). To cater for such readers you must include some of your information in a form that they can digest.

Finally, you have those wonderful people who actually read what you write! However, even they will start with a scan, before deciding to read on from start to finish.

## Capture feeling and emotion

Sometimes you will be asked to write on a subject that is more than a little dull. I have read some gripping features on the dullest subjects, as well as many dreary articles on potentially mind-blowing topics. Whatever you are writing about, write with feeling. Depending on the article, ensure your enthusiasm, empathy, anger, sadness, happiness … comes across. Let it infect your reader.

## The end

So far we have looked at how to open an article, how to break it into readable chunks, and how to give it a theme. But what about the ending? Some people find that stopping can be every bit as difficult as starting. Articles should have a nice, rounded ending: abrupt, sudden closures are a sign of the inexperienced writer. If you have developed a clear theme or hypothesis through your article, you will reach an end quite naturally. If not, here are some ideas for bringing your article to a conclusion:

● A look to the future – a short muse about the future trends of what you are writing about can round off an article
● A conclusion that refers back to your opening paragraph
● A rhetorical question to leave the reader thinking

Start powerfully, round off neatly, and fill the middle with interesting prose. That's the secret of a good article.

# 16 Staff and customer newsletters

Many companies produce staff and customer newsletters. Too many are little more than company propaganda, and are discarded unread by a sceptical audience. This chapter shows how to put together a really readable newsletter. It suggests story ideas and shows how to mix long and short pieces.

This chapter covers both internal publications (for staff) and external ones (for customers). Although a staff newsletter is a different beast to a customer newsletter, the same principles apply.

## Staff newsletters

Customer newsletters are very clearly viewed as marketing tools. Sadly many staff newsletters are seen as 'human resources' or personnel tools. Although there is debate about this, my view is that staff newsletters should be regarded as a marketing production. You are 'selling' your company to staff. You want their loyalty and understanding. You want their interest and attention. In other words, you want from your staff all that you want from your customers.

That said, you have to be careful not to produce something that is regarded as nothing more than company propaganda. A one-way vehicle for the bosses to spout the company line at a disbelieving and cynical staff will do you no favours. An upbeat newsletter full of success stories will not wash with staff who are demotivated or threatened with redundancy. Staff newsletters have to be brave. They must not shirk from addressing difficult or delicate issues and from breaking bad news honestly. Nor must they be afraid to present differing viewpoints on the same issue, so that important topics are properly debated. Only then will they win the respect of staff and attract a strong readership.

Here's an example of the sort of corporate propaganda that you should avoid:

---

**ZIPCO WELL PLACED FOR FUTURE GROWTH**
A planned restructuring at Zipco will leave the company well placed to tap into new markets and to grow from strength to strength. That is the view of chairman Bob Zip, who today unveiled exciting plans for the company's future.

---

> 'We are in a highly competitive market,' said Mr Zip, 'but this reorganization will ensure that we are fit for the task ahead. Part of the restructuring will involve downsizing of around 50 per cent, making us leaner and fitter.'

What at first appears to be good news for staff is actually dreadful. Half the workforce is to be sacked! It is hopeless trying to wrap this up as something good; people are not stupid. False corporate optimism of this sort breeds anger and resentment among staff. Be upfront with bad news, however unpalatable, if you want your staff to believe what they read in their newsletter.

### Content

What you put in depends on the company, its size, whether it has more than one base, etc. What's right for a multinational's newsletter will not always be right for a tiny business. Here are some things you might like to consider:

- News – any developments and how they will affect the company's performance and the staff
- Staff news – promotions and moves
- Letters page – to make it a two-way vehicle
- Articles – more in-depth looks at certain issues
- Rules/requirements – anything staff should know about, such as the introduction of a no-smoking policy or other procedures that will affect them
- Information – about holiday closing, for example
- Open space – a chance for staff to sound off about something

### What you should avoid

- A chairperson's or chief executive's message
- Departmental profiles – unless they are written in a lively way and are likely to be read with interest by staff in other areas
- Badly drawn and boring cartoon strips
- Over-simple crosswords and puzzles

## Customer newsletters

Many customer newsletters are of the 'Aren't we Great' variety. They tell the customer how fantastic the company is, how wonderful its equipment or procedures are, how great the staff are, how superb the customer service is ... Customers could not care less! No one is going to read company hype and puffery. Your readers are not stupid. They will not swallow wholesale anything you put in print. They have no interest in you, only in what you can do for them.

Customer newsletters should do at least one of the following:

- Inform in a way that is relevant and interesting
- Promote your products – but not too obviously
- Sell – softly
- Establish/maintain a relationship

To get customer newsletters read (that is, after all, the objective!), they have to be worth reading. Newsletters written from a company perspective will never be read. Only those which take the customer's viewpoint stand a chance. So don't say how great your products are, show how they can help or have helped your customers. Take the following example, starting with an illustration of how not to do it:

> ✗ **HAYES SECURITY PRODUCTS** [article accompanied by photo of Hayes chief executive]
> Hayes is *the* name in home security, providing burglar alarms, window locks, door chains, spy-holes, entry phones, even CCTV. Our pedigree stretches back over a century, yet we work with leading edge technology. Hayes is an industry leader in security products, supplying over half the UK's window locks. Indeed we are the industry's most admired supplier ...

This may all be true, but so what? It's not going to hook your readers. They want something that will interest them, that will connect with their own experience, that will mean something to them. The following article promotes Hayes security products in a more interesting, gripping way:

> ✔ **As burglary rates soar, we show you how to keep burglars at bay.** [Article accompanied by photo of woman in ransacked house, looking distressed]

> **SAFE AS HOUSES?**
>
> It's everyone's worst nightmare. You get back from holiday and find your home's been trashed. Papers everywhere. Furniture upturned. Even the kids' playroom ransacked. This is the scene Jenny Smith from Windsor found when she got back from a fortnight in the Algarve. Her home had been burgled and all her jewellery stolen. She lost a cameo brooch left to her by her mother, her eternity ring, all her gold, her christening bracelet, the lot. Gone forever.
>
> 'For months I dreaded leaving the house, even for a few minutes,' says Jenny. 'I became paranoid. It was affecting my health. Eventually I got round to doing something about it. The local Crime Prevention Officer came round and suggested that I get some improved home security – burglar alarm, window locks, that kind of thing. So I did. I had a Hayes Home Protector fitted and it's the best thing I ever did. Now I sleep at night. I leave the house and don't worry about what I'll find when I get back. It may sound over the top to say that it has changed my life for the better, but it really has,' says Jenny.
>
> If you want to know how you can improve your home's security cheaply and quickly, see the article on page 4 …

This sort of approach clicks with readers. They can identify with the woman featured, feel sympathy with her, put themselves in her shoes. It gets them thinking. Maybe they should improve their home security. Perhaps they will read that helpful article on page 4. Then they might use the money-off vouchers mailed with the newsletter to buy some of your products. You've made a sale by being interesting and informative. You would not have done it by being trumpet-blowing or too 'corporate'.

*Content*

This depends on your company, products and readership. What will appeal for a business-to-business readership will be different to a consumer newsletter. Consider the following:

- Different/unusual ways of using the product – e.g. recipes using your baked beans; things you can make using your glue; interior design paint effects which can be achieved using your products
- Helpful hints
- 'How to' features – how to get a bigger pension, how to transform junk furniture

- Case histories/human interest
- Seasonal stories – Christmas, Easter, summer hols, etc.
- Your questions answered
- Feedback and what we'll do as a result
- Calendar/forthcoming events – new season's clothes arrive, fashion show, summer sale, open day

## Style

Every newsletter should have a writing style that shows its personality. It might be:

- Friendly/chatty
- Helpful
- Informative
- Authoritative

Decide on style and stick to it. Ensure the design reinforces the style. An informal, chatty newsletter should look different from a more serious, authoritative one.

## Cover page

Every cover page should have a lead article accompanied, if possible, by a strong photograph. The lead article should have a bold headline that attracts attention. Combined, these three features should be enough to make people want to pick up the newsletter. If you want tips on how the lead story, headline and photo work together, pick up any newspaper. See how they do it. Consider a contents box too. Even if your newsletter is just four pages long, it can still include one. This serves to draw the reader in and get them to open up the newsletter. Getting your front page right is so important. If it looks unattractive or uninviting, your reader is unlikely to look beyond it.

## Other points to consider

You want your reader to get to know your publication and to look forward to receiving it. If each newsletter looks completely different from the last, you may find yourself starting from scratch in building up a following. Aim for familiarity, so readers recognize your newsletter, but keep it fresh too. Try to have regular features so that readers get to know their way about the newsletter. Use a familiar design and layout too.

The ideal newsletter contains a mix of stories. Some are short snippets, others lengthier features that can delve into an issue. Some are light-hearted, others serious. This mix gives the newsletter pace and helps cater for the different needs of readers.

You might find that articles are submitted for you to use in the newsletter. More often than not they will benefit from editing or even complete rewriting. Don't be feeble when it comes to the red pen. You must ensure that anything making it into print is worthy of it. If rubbish is submitted, you must edit it. You might upset the writer, but that's better than inflicting substandard copy on all your readers and damaging your newsletter's reputation.

# 17 Annual reports

Thankfully many company reports are a great deal better these days than they were in the past. There are, though, plenty which leave a great deal of room for improvement. This chapter will show how to produce exciting, different, mould-breaking, lively and effective annual reports that actually get read.

All too often the production of the annual report is regarded as a chore. This shows. Rather than a carefully planned, well-written and readable report, one is presented with a dreary account of an organization's activities, followed by pages of unintelligible figures. It need not be like this.

Annual reports have two main types of reader:

1  *Those with a professional interest:* there are some poor souls who have to read annual reports, however dry and dull. This group includes, for example, bankers and City analysts.
2  *Those with a passing interest:* this might include shareholders, staff, and others receiving a report. They have some interest in the company and will flick through a report, but you'll need to persuade them to give it more than a glance.

Your job is to satisfy the professional reader (and their need for the nitty-gritty of the year's activities) and also to interest the 'amateur'. Achieving this is not always easy, but it can be done. If you can finance it, why not produce two reports:

- A full annual report and accounts (for the professionals)
- An abridged report (for others), which includes an advert for the full version

By producing two reports you can tailor the copy for the reader. Each gets what they want, in a form that they can digest. If the production of two reports is not feasible, try splitting the report in two. Keep it interesting and lively at the front, with all the statutory stuff at the back. That way everyone's happy.

As well as satisfying your various audiences, you must fulfil certain legal requirements. These requirements vary depending on whether you are:

- A public listed company
- An unlisted company

- A small company (this is based on turnover, number of staff and balance sheet)
- A charity (there are varying requirements for different types of charity, depending on their status and on whether they are also limited companies. Additionally there are differences for Scottish charities)

It would be impossible here to go into the various requirements, which are governed by legislation (such as the Companies Act 1985, Statements of Standard Accounting Practice, Statement of Recommended Practice Accounting by Charities, etc.). While many of the requirements relate to the figures in annual accounts, some concern the narrative. You might, for example (depending on the status of your company or organization), be required to:

- Include a Chairperson's statement
- Include directors' reports
- Disclose certain information about future activities, research and development, and other plans
- Include activities and results

Talk to your company secretary (if you have one) or to your auditors to establish the requirements for your organization.

Most reports follow a formula. They start with a chairperson's report, followed by a series of statements by the chief executive, the finance director and other directors. Inevitably this approach is dull, disjointed, and often leads to repetition. A way around this is to develop a theme for the report. Explain the theme to each director and ask them to tell you about progress around this theme during the year. Gather the raw data from them, then turn it into flowing copy that hangs together. Ensure each director's report links with the next one, yet avoids boring repetition.

Be confident about your report writing. Just because most reports are rather staid productions, there's no need for yours to be. Don't be a slave to convention: let your creativity dictate how the report should be. If your company makes clothes, why not produce a report that looks like a fashion magazine? Try to break the mould and produce something that makes people sit up and notice.

An annual report will be a key publication for a whole year, so it is worth spending time getting it right. Time, alas, is the thing lacking in so many reports. They are hurried and it shows. Take your time with a report. Start at least six months before publication date if you want a comfortable schedule. Think through ideas and themes. Try them out on others. Start planning the content and letting the report take shape. Timely planning will save on tears later on.

As with virtually any copywriting assignment, get hold of the work of others. Look at their reports and study the content, style, design, the presentation of financial information. See what you like and what you can adapt. Make a note of what to avoid. Be sparked by others' ideas. Take them a stage further and mould ideas into your own.

One of the greatest challenges of annual reports and accounts is to present the accounts section in a way that is meaningful to the average reader. It might be crystal clear to the accountants and auditors, but most people give up when faced with complex balance sheets. If you want your finances understood, present them so they make sense. Enhance the balance sheet with user-friendly charts and graphics, attractively designed, to show at a glance what the figures mean. Or add a plain English commentary to explain the finances.

Another perceived challenge is that of cramming a year's work into a few pages. In fact there's no challenge at all. You should never try to cram it all in. Select the key highlights and turn them into a read-able flavour. That's better than packing pages with every last detail, regardless of whether or not it will be read.

As if that were not enough challenges, here's another: how do you deal with the inevitable lists that most reports contain? How can you make them interesting? Easy. Delete unnecessary lists, then add a bit of life to any that remain. Give the lists meaning. For example, say you are listing all the board members or directors. Don't just state their names, add a little interest by telling the reader something about the people behind the names. Don't write:

> ✗ John Smith
> Mary Taylor
> Rajiv Ram

write:

> ✔ **John Smith**
> As well as serving on our Board, John is also a director of Jeeve's Champagne. You will see that this year we have introduced champagne truffles to our range of luxury chocolates, thanks to John's links with Jeeve's.
> **Mary Taylor**
> Food writer Mary Taylor has sat on our Board for ten years ...

Although the annual report and accounts is a legal requirement for many, you can use it as a marketing tool. It should present your image, inform, educate, persuade, reassure, motivate, impress. As a copywriter you need to think about how you can turn the raw information about your company's performance into a powerful and persuasive document. You can achieve this by:

- Lively and readable copy
- Lots of bite-size chunks of copy (as opposed to dense text)
- Great photos and good design
- Good use of captions
- Being outward-looking, not inward-looking
- Focusing on what your products do, not how they came about
- Adding human interest

If your report is to work as a marketing tool, it must help differentiate you from your competitors. That means that it must encapsulate what you stand for as a company. Copy and design need to work together to convey your organization's philosophy, personality and principles. Yes, you need to give a snapshot of the year, but you need to show how that relates to past years and to future years. You must leave the reader with a real feel for what you are about, and an interest in finding out more next year.

# 18 Catalogues

All copywriting assignments require planning, but none more so than the catalogue. This chapter shows you how to plan a catalogue and how to write catalogue entries that sell products.

It is fair to say that all marketing material should be regarded as selling tools, even if the selling is just of an image or an idea. The catalogue is the supreme selling tool, in the most upfront way. It has to do the job of the sales assistant, singing the virtues of a product. And as the product is not in front of the potential customer, it has to do what it can to make up for this deficiency. It must achieve all this with just a few words and pictures, and to do it persuasively enough to get people to part with their money. What a challenge for the copywriter!

Essentially there are four types of catalogue:

- *Descriptive* – this type shows the goods and offers a straightforward description of the product, limiting itself largely to the essentials, such as size, colour, materials, etc. A typical entry might read:

> **Polo shirt**
> 100% cotton. Navy, white and black. Sizes S, M, L, XL. Machine washable.
> £16.99

- *Descriptive plus* – like the above, such catalogues offer the necessary description. Although catalogue entries tend to be brief, these offer a little more than the basic minimum. Generally a little persuasive sales patter is thrown in to enhance the description. For example:

> **Polo shirt**
> A classic that no man's wardrobe should be without. Our polo shirt features authentic rib collar and cuffs (often omitted on cheaper imposters) and quality top-stitching to create a more robust garment. 100% cotton. Navy, white and black. Sizes S, M, L, XL. Machine washable.
> £16.99

- *Magalogue* – this is a cross between a catalogue and a magazine. It has articles as well as catalogue entries, providing the shopper with more of a read. It might include features on some of the designers whose clothing or goods are featured in the catalogue, or perhaps on the countries where the items come from. Some magalogues even feature guest writers. Its aim is to interact more with the reader and to make them feel more involved with the products.
- *Specialogue* – this is a very specialist catalogue catering for a niche market and offering specialist products.

The trend, particularly with more upmarket catalogues, is towards the magalogue. Certainly they offer more scope for the copywriter. Even if the products in the catalogue are quite ordinary, interesting, relevant and readable features can be included to add a bit of fizz. For example, a menswear catalogue carried a feature on the button-down shirt, full of 1950s and 1960s nostalgia, complete with photos of pop group The Who, and other icons of that era. A tile manufacturer carried articles in their catalogue by experts writing on historic Moorish, Islamic and Victorian tiles. Not only can you enliven a catalogue in this way, you can also add credibility to your own goods. If experts are willing to write in your catalogue on rare Islamic tiles, doesn't that say something about the standing of your own tiles?

Catalogues which feature more than just the products add value for the reader. You are giving them more than just a hard sell. You are sharing knowledge, useful hints and tips, expertise. Your catalogue is giving them something extra.

When writing a catalogue, first decide on what type to go for. Will you do a straight descriptive job, or is a magalogue more relevant? Your choice depends on what you are selling, how you wish to position your company, and also on budget. Do you have to cram 1000 products into 24 pages? If so, there will be no space for features.

Now to planning. How will you organize it? Catalogues need to have a logical order, and it's up to you to come up with one. For example, if you were writing a clothing catalogue, would you organize it under menswear, women's wear and children's clothing? Or according to garment type (trousers, shoes, coats, etc.)? Or a combination of these? Or would you go for a different classification altogether? You cannot begin to write until you are clear on the structure.

Now decide what to include (in addition to product descriptions). Will you feature articles? If so, what on? Do you need to include instructions on how to order, how to measure, how to get refunds? An index? An order form? Draw up a list so that you don't forget anything.

Then you need to consider how to convey confidence in your company or charity. If you are already a household name, this is not such an issue. But customers considering ordering from an unknown will be looking for proof that you are *bona fide*. Include some soothing words to reassure, mention any guarantees and money-back offers, and anything else that will calm customers. You might also want to include a little something about the company or charity, such as how long you have been trading or (in the case of charity catalogue) what work you do and how the profits will be spent.

Go back and check that you have included everything relevant and necessary, such as addresses and phone numbers. If something important is missing, you will lose sales, so be thorough in your check.

When it comes to writing the catalogue you need, as with anything you write, to consider your audience and arrive at a suitable style that will satisfy them and position your company correctly. Your buyers should know who your customers are. Find out as much as you can about them so you can be sure to hit the right note with your copy. If your buyers have done a good job in selecting the right goods at the right price, if your marketing people have targeted well, if your designer has made everything look attractive – and you have produced persuasive copy – you'll see the fruits of your work in the sales you make. That's the real test of whether or not you have got it right.

# 19 Leaflets

Leaflets lie at the less glamorous end of copywriting. Annual reports and glossy brochures are regarded as important pieces of company literature (even if sometimes they are not given quite the attention they deserve), but the humble leaflet is so often – quite unjustifiably – relegated to the bottom of the list. This chapter resurrects the leaflet to its rightful place as an important marketing tool. It looks at the different types of leaflet and how to produce one with bite.

Leaflets, because they are cheaper to produce than glossy brochures and catalogues, often have a wider distribution. They are given away more readily and so larger numbers find their way into circulation. As a result, they are very important pieces of marketing material. Often they are the first point of contact a potential customer will have with you. After seeing one of your leaflets, the reader might request a brochure, then a sales visit, then make a purchase. If the leaflet fails to do its job properly, the would-be customer will not progress along the line to make a sale. So producing a quality leaflet is important.

One of the greatest challenges a leaflet poses for the copywriter is that by its nature it is short, generally no more than a couple of sides of A4 – but often just half that! Allowing for photos, illustrations and 'white space' you may find yourself left with room for just 400–500 words – less still on an A5 leaflet. (To give you an indication of how long that is, this and the above two paragraphs come to well over 300 words.) It's tough trying to fit it all into so few words. Every word counts. Every illustration must add information. To get away with it you need to focus on two or three key points. Everything else must be omitted.

To help you focus in on the key points, you need to be clear about what type of leaflet you are writing. Most leaflets fall into one of the following four categories:

- General-purpose leaflets
- Information leaflets
- Sales leaflets
- Booking leaflets

*General-purpose leaflets*

A general-purpose leaflet looks very broadly at what you do as a company or organization. It can be difficult trying to cover everything you do without getting too wordy. Sometimes the best approach is simply to try to present a flavour of what you do rather than go into the detail, so that the reader is left feeling that they would like to do business with you. They don't need to know everything about you in order to feel good about you. You can refer to brochures and catalogues you produce, should they want further information.

### Information leaflets

Leaflets created to inform (e.g. 'All your insurance questions answered' or 'The benefits of smokeless fuel') are often the easiest to write. The 'questions and answers' format works best here – you ask the questions that the reader will want addressed, then go on to answer them. It's as simple as that. A question is also a good device for the front cover, e.g. 'Want to know more about home insulation?'.

### Sales leaflets

For a sales leaflet to sell, it must contain a call to action or a mechanism to enable easy response. This might be in the form of an order form or a coupon – or simply the inclusion of your address, opening hours and directions, if appropriate.

### Booking leaflets

These are leaflets designed to publicize and encourage booking for a conference, training course, special event or similar. You should aim to make such leaflets as easy to reply to as possible. The tear-off slip is a good device here, but if you are using one make sure that you:

(a)  Include the return address on it
(b)  Don't put any essential information on the back
(c)  Include a cut-off date for applications/bookings

Once you have decided on the purpose of the leaflet, you can make a start at writing it.

## The front cover

People do judge books (and leaflets!) by their covers. Make sure yours is arresting, if you want to stand a chance of your leaflet being read. Design, of course, plays a vital role in shaping the impact of a leaflet. But copy, too, is crucial when it comes to attracting that all-important attention. Think carefully about how you approach the front cover. The wrong choice of words on the front cover could spell disaster for your company. It could switch off your intended readership and lose you valuable custom. Take this fictitious example, the front cover of a leaflet promoting a new modem aimed at small businesses:

> ✗ Presenting the new H17i. Our best modem yet.

This *might* attract the interest of people on the lookout for a modem. It will not hold any interest for people who do not realize that a modem would be a real boon to their business. However, the approach below would do the trick:

> ✔ Would you like to know:
> ● How to send faxes without a fax machine?
> ● How to send data without using a courier?
> ● How to slash your national and international phone bill?
>
> [use the inside of the leaflet to explain that these are some of the many things a modem allows you to do]

As you can see, such an approach enables you to catch the interest of people who are not considering a modem purchase. It offers you a chance to persuade them, by talking in their language and recognizing their needs.

Your front cover must achieve a dual purpose. First, it must attract attention, so that the leaflet is noticed and picked up. Next, it must foster interest, so that the leaflet is opened up and read. The approach you take with your front cover depends on the subject of your leaflet. If you are sharing with people the secrets of eternal youth, or twenty ways to get rich quick, chances are that you will have little trouble in attracting the necessary attention and fostering interest. All you need write on the front cover of the leaflet is:

> The Secrets of Eternal Youth

or

> Twenty Ways to Get Rich Quick

The subject matter is powerful enough to do the work for you. But what if you are selling life insurance, pension plans, or other less 'sexy' subjects? Leaflets headed:

Life Insurance

or

Pension Plans

are unlikely to produce the desired effect – unless the reader is actively seeking those products. So you need to find a different way of capturing the interest of your reader. There are two techniques that can work well: being cryptic and using ellipses. For example, take the life insurance leaflet:

[front cover]
In the time it takes you to read this ...

[inside the leaflet]
... over 100 people in Britain will have died. Less than half of them will have had life insurance.

Now for the pension plan leaflet:

[front cover]
Foreign travel. A home in the country. A decent income. No cares or worries.

[inside the leaflet]
Is this how you will be spending your retirement? Without a good pension plan, life after 60 could be very different. Poverty. A cold and damp home. Struggling to pay the bills. Which scenario would you prefer?

Both of these leaflets lure the reader. The front cover is interesting, unlike a direct appeal to take out a pension or insurance. Each enables the reader to consider the drawbacks of life without these products.

*Which format?*

It is a good idea, when producing a leaflet, to know its format before you begin to write. That way you can plan your blocks of text to fit the space. The majority of leaflets are:

- A4 landscape folded in half (i.e. four pages of A5)
- A4 landscape folded twice (i.e. six pages each of which is a third of A4)
- A5

Of course, leaflets can be printed on larger or smaller sheets, and you can have them folded in all sorts of fancy ways. Select the format that is best for the amount of copy you have, and that fits the budget. Then plan your copy around it.

# 20 Everything else!

This final chapter deals with a range of small writing assignments that do not merit a chapter to themselves, important as they are. Find out how to write clear instructions, how to write for foreigners, how to write coupons and response mechanisms ... and lots more.

## Coupons and response mechanisms

When writing adverts, direct mail, leaflets and various other items of marketing material, you may need to produce some form of coupon or response mechanism. Bear the following points in mind when drawing up your coupon response:

1 Put your address on the coupon rather than in the body of the advertisement/leaflet. (If a reader loses the advert or brochure having cut off the coupon, they will still know where to send it.)
2 If you are using coupons in different publications, code the coupon in the bottom corner so you can tell where it was cut out from. That way you can monitor response to your advert, and assess which publication produced the best response; this is essential if you plan to advertise again.
3 Leave enough space. Make sure the coupon is big enough for respondents to complete with ease – if they have to squash their details in they may give up, or you may have trouble reading their writing.
4 Ensure you word it so that you elicit all the information you need or want from your respondent.
5 Ensure that you repeat the offer, e.g. 'Yes, please rush me a copy of your free brochure ...'.

## Instructions

Recall the frustrations of assembling flat pack furniture. The pieces never seem to fit together, and the instructions appear not to relate to the assorted components before you. Writing clear and easy-to-follow instructions can be tricky, but you make your task easier if you follow the simple steps below:

1 Break down the activity into simple numbered steps
2 Include as many of the following as appropriate:
   ● A simple checklist
   ● A list of the contents

- Say how long it will take
- A troubleshooting guide
- A clear and carefully labelled diagram identifying the various parts referred to in the instructions (but be sure to use the same labels in the text as in the diagram, e.g. don't refer to 'Board A' in the text, when it is labelled 'Piece A' in the diagram)

3. Aim for clarity and brevity. If you can shorten sentences by cutting out any unnecessary words, do so. For example, don't write:

> ✗ Take the piece labelled 'a' on the enclosed diagram and attach it (using the screwdriver provided) to piece 'b'

Write:

> ✔ Screw piece B to piece A.

4 Once you've written the instructions, get someone to follow them
5 Amend instructions in the light of any exposed ambiguity or lack of clarity
6 Be as precise as you can to avoid doubt. Don't write

> ✗ Place in a hot oven

write:

> ✔ Place in an oven preheated to 220 degrees Centigrade

## Packaging

A product's packaging (box or carton, labels, etc.) represents a great marketing opportunity for the copywriter. Too often packaging is seen as a design challenge: you should regard it as shared terrain, with you and the designer or packaging specialist working together. It's true that attractive packaging can sell a product. I'm a sucker for anything that comes in a glittery box. But the words on that packaging are important too. Depending on your product, and where it is being sold, there are legislative requirements that you will need to comply with. You may need to list:

- Ingredients
- Country of manufacture
- Weight
- Nutritional information
- Materials
- 'CE' kitemark and other accreditations
- Warnings (e.g. 'Keep away from naked flames')
- Contents
- Address
- Guarantee

Aside from these statutory requirements, there's the opportunity for some creativity. The challenge is to write some appealing prose that will fit neatly into the small space available on a label or box. Note the word 'appealing'. There's little point in simply stating what's inside, do a bit of sales patter. Here's an example of how not to do it:

✗ Six bars of glycerine soap, each in a different colour

You should write something a little more engaging, such as:

✔ Six bars of pure glycerine soap – all the colours of the rainbow. Made by monks in the Alyserian hills, using traditional techniques that have not changed since the time of Jesus. Pure, clean and refreshing.

It's the same soap, but now it sounds a more interesting proposition. There's a bit of history attached to it. Of course, it is easier to write colourful copy for interesting products. What if you are writing packaging for motor oil, nuts and bolts, or spanners? The same rule applies: make the product sound interesting. Take the example of the spanner. Don't just write:

✗ This pack contains two domestic grade spanners suitable for DIY use write:

> ✔ Two spanners ideal for DIY. Booker's Spanners are made of top grade steel (the same steel we use for our 'Professional' range), so they won't rust and are guaranteed to provide years of trouble-free use.

You can see that packaging is not simply a device to list contents, it's an opportunity to persuade and to sell.

## Captions

Earlier in this book I looked at the use of captions in adverts. But it is not only in advertising that a writer should pay particular attention to captions. In every piece of marketing material you produce where captions are involved, you should write them with as much thought as you give the body copy. Too often, captions (to illustrations and photographs) are added as an afterthought. They should be regarded as an integral part of the copy. Indeed, they are far more likely to be read than the body copy, so their role is vital. Clearly a caption that merely repeats what the illustration shows is a wasted opportunity. The role of the caption is to add information, not repeat it. Suppose you were carrying a photograph of the footballer Paul Gascoigne in your marketing material. You would be mad to caption it just:

> ✘ Paul Gascoigne

Far better to make the most of the opportunity with something like:

> ✔ Top footballer Paul Gascoigne insists on the best. That's why he wears Hi-Star trainers on and off the field.

Do not feel that your caption must be short – just two or three words. Extended captions can be used to good effect, running to three or even four sentences.

## Notices

Most notices make two mistakes. They:

> ● Have too much text
> ● Lack an attention-grabbing headline

Don't make these mistakes yourself. So instead of writing:

> ✗ We would like our customers to note that batches of Bobby's Babyfood bought at this store during April may contain small pieces of rubber, due to equipment failure at the manufacturers. If you have bought any Bobby's Babyfood at this store in April, please return it to us for a full refund. Under no circumstances should you use the product. We apologize for any alarm or inconvenience. If you have any questions or concerns, please ask any member of staff if you can speak to the store manager.

write:

> ✔ **URGENT PRODUCT RECALL**
> **Bobby's Babyfood**
>
> If you bought Bobby's Babyfood at this store during April, please return it to us immediately as it may contain pieces of rubber. You will be given a full refund. We apologize for any alarm or inconvenience this recall may cause. Please ask to see the store manager if you have any questions or concerns.

The second version attracts attention with its main headline and narrows the audience with the secondary headline. It is less wordy and thus clearer.

## Posters

Many of the rules for notices apply to posters too. Keep it brief, bold and simple. Use a strong and attention-grabbing headline. Include all the pertinent information, or details of how to find out more. You don't have to use complete sentences. For example, do not write:

> ✗ **CRANBERRY'S CARNIVAL**
>
> Cranberry's Department store is delighted to announce that its traditional annual carnival will take place again this year. As usual there will be plenty for the whole family, with fairground rides, pony rides, stalls, food and lots more besides. So be there for the event of the year.
>
> **Village Green, Billington. Saturday 24 May**
> **from 2 pm to 5 pm.**

Instead write:

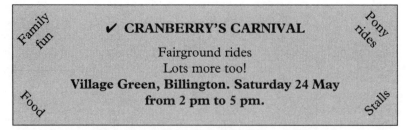

It is easier to take in a few words than to digest full sentences, particularly when read at a distance or on the move, as most posters will be.

## Speech-writing

Most of what you write will be read silently. Not so the speech; speeches are, of course, written to be read aloud. That makes them a very different proposition from, say, a press advert or a brochure. Although you should try to capture the informality and vitality of the spoken word in every copywriting assignment, nowhere is this more true than when writing a speech. We can all recall tortured speeches that were as painful for the audience as for the speaker. Stilted or awkward phrases delivered with a monotonous voice are guaranteed to produce yawns from listeners, if not snores! How can you avoid this?

- Remember that your writing will be read out loud, so use ordinary language that you would speak when holding a conversation
- Write in a style appropriate for the speaker. Do not use words or phrases that they would not use
- Adopt a style that will suit the audience and the event – a humorous speech at a rather stuffy event might be out of place (or it might be a refreshing change)
- Use humour with care and expertise: there is nothing worse than jokes that no one laughs at, allusions no one understands, and wit that causes embarrassment

## Writing for foreigners

Most foreigners are not fluent in English. So if you are asked to write something that will be read by foreigners (such as information leaflets for hotels, tourist information material, or publicity for an international exhibition) then bear the following points in mind:

---

- If someone's first language is not English, they are unlikely to understand colloquialisms, slang and abbreviations
- They are likely to find shorter words and sentences easier
- They may be using a dictionary to aid translation (so try to select words that do not have too many possible meanings)
- Clichés may be taken literally (e.g. it's raining cats and dogs)

---

# Appendix: Improvement in writing ability

In the first chapter you were asked to assess your writing ability by completing a quick questionnaire. Now let's see if you are any happier with your copywriting skills than you were when you started this book. If you have read the book thoroughly, taken on board the tips and worked through the exercises, you should find that you are much more confident and capable.

Complete the questionnaire again. Then compare the results with the questionnaire you filled in at the front of the book.

1   I would rate my writing ability as:
   (a)   Poor
   (b)   Slightly below average
   (c)   Average
   (d)   Slightly above average
   (e)   Good
   (f)   Excellent

2   I find getting started:
   (a)   Almost impossible
   (b)   Very difficult
   (c)   Quite difficult
   (d)   Hard but not insurmountable
   (e)   Reasonably easy
   (f)   Very easy

3   When I am asked to write some marketing material I feel:
   (a)   A sense of dread and/or panic
   (b)   Worried that I will not be able to do a good job of it
   (c)   That it will be a struggle, but I will be able to come up with something, however second-rate
   (d)   That I will do an OK job, but not a great one
   (e)   That I will be able to produce a good piece of work
   (f)   That it will be a doddle and the output will be great

4   I think that the marketing material I write is:
   (a)   Dreadful
   (b)   Poor
   (c)   Average
   (d)   Good but could be improved
   (e)   Above average
   (f)   Excellent

5   When it comes to words and language:
   (a)  I have no interest in words and how they work – indeed I never give words so much as a passing thought
   (b)  I'm not that interested in words, but very occasionally I will look at an ad or brochure and wonder how they came up with the concept
   (c)  I have an average interest in words – no more and no less than an average marketing person
   (d)  I often look at/analyse/think about other people's creative work
   (e)  I love reading and thinking about professional copy and find myself doing it all the time
   (f)  I am very interested in words, indeed I find language fascinating

6   When it comes to writing marketing material (sales letters, press ads, brochures, annual reports):
   (a)  I find it difficult to write anything
   (b)  I can write some types of marketing material to a reasonable standard, but find others more difficult
   (c)  I can write most types of material, but there's room for improvement across the board
   (d)  I am confident that I can tackle most assignments without too much difficulty and can produce good work
   (e)  I can tackle all assignments and produce good work
   (f)  I can turn my hand to anything with ease, always producing very good work

7   How long does it take you to write, say, a one-page sales letter, or some other short piece of marketing material, to a good standard?
   (a)  It takes me far far too long to get material written – perhaps three times too long
   (b)  It takes me longer than it should – perhaps twice as long
   (c)  I take a little longer than I should
   (d)  I am fairly quick, but I could be a bit faster
   (e)  I can produce good work faster than the average person
   (f)  I can turn out quality work quickly

## Scores

Now add up your score. Award yourself:
One point for every (a) you ticked
Two for every (b)
Three for a (c)

Four for a (d)
Five for an (e)
Six for an (f)

## Assessment

Refer back to page 7. Read the paragraph that refers to your score. You should find an improved score. Hopefully, after seeing how much you have improved you will gain in confidence and take on more demanding copywriting assignments. The more you do, and the more you are taxed, the better you will become. The better you become, the more you will enjoy writing and the more you will want to take on. By this stage you will have developed your own style and will write quite naturally and a lot less painfully. Keep it up, then, and that day will be just round the corner. Good luck!

# Index